Maritime Topics for English Learners

| Mi-Lim Ryoo |

KM KYUNG MOON SA

PREFACE

This book is intended to be used in English classes for students who have a special interest in maritime topics. It introduces students to a variety of maritime subjects and to Maritime English as a special case of English for Specific Purposes.

Level

The book is intended mainly for elementary students who are new to the study of maritime science, business, literature, and so on. It concentrates on common topics that the student may encounter later on in the workplace.

How the book is organized

The book consists of 12 units. Each unit focuses on a particular maritime-related theme. For the list of units, see the Contents on the following pages.

Each unit has two reading passages, with Vocabulary on the same page. Right after each reading passage are Vocabulary Check and Reading Comprehension question. At the back of the book are the Answers to the questions.

How to use the book

The units are essentially free-standanding and are not ordered by content or difficulty. This means that students may work through the book in any order.

Acknowledgements

I would like to acknowledge my colleagues, Se-Eun Jhang, Gun-Su Lee, Jong-Jin Noh, Ok-Sook Hong, Kevin Parent, and Mark L. Wing, and especially Wendell R. Pepperdine for their contributions to the early version of this book.

CONTENTS

Unit 1. Oceans 1

Origins of the Oceans 2

The Five Oceans 6

Unit 2. Ocean Life 11

Marine Habitats 12

Marine versus Land Mammals 16

Unit 3. Maritime History 23

Great Explorers 24

Pirates 29

Unit 4. Ships / Navigation 35

Talking about Ships 36

Nautical Charts 42

Unit 5. Ports and Port Management 49

History of Ports 50

Port Authorities 54

Unit 6. Maritime Law 59

Law of the Sea 60

Captain Goes down with the Ship 64

Unit 7. Navy / Coast Guard 69

Battle of Myeongnyang 70
Coast Guard 74

Unit 8. Fisheries / Fishing 81

Aquaculture 82
Food Chain at Sea 86

Unit 9. Sea Commerce 93

Container Ships 94
Shipping and the Economy 98

Unit. 10. Cruise Industry 105

History of Cruise Ships 106
Growth of Cruise Ships 110

Unit. 11. Maritime Disasters 115

Typhoons 116
Taean Oil Spill 120

Unit. 12. Maritime Literature 125

Moby Dick 126
Kon-Tiki 130

Questions & Answers 135

Unit 1

Oceans

Have you ever pondered how the ocean was formed, how big it is, how the ocean is differentiated from the sea, and so on? The goals of this unit are to provide some answers to the questions you might have pertaining to the ocean and to make you more familiar with it.

The assignment in this unit is to research on seas and write the name and location of seas.

Oceans

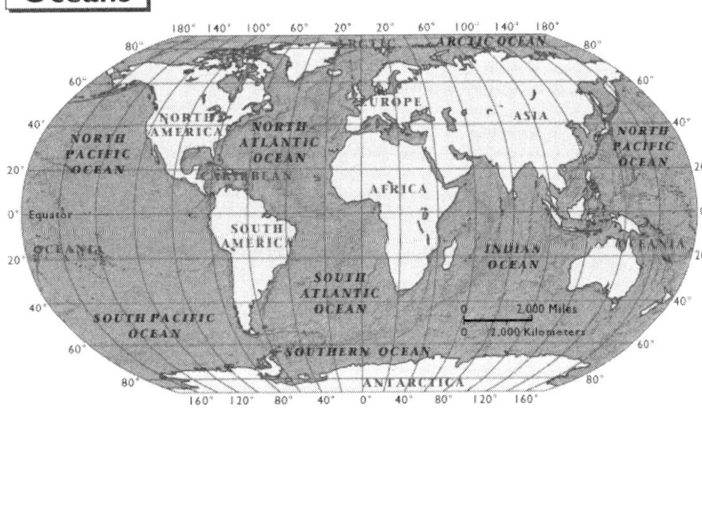

Origins of the Oceans

Earth formed about 4.6 billion years ago by collisions in the giant disc-shaped cloud of dust and gas that also formed the sun. At the early stages of formation, the earth appeared as a cold body in space, containing all of the chemical elements known in Nature. The **atmosphere** and **hydrosphere** did not yet exist; the surface of the planet was completely lifeless. But gradually, due to **gravitational** forces, energy released by the breakdown of **radioactive** elements and lunar tides, the core of the earth began to heat up.

When temperatures near the core of the earth reached the level where the melting of **iron oxides** and other compounds could occur, the active processes began for the formation of a **nucleus** and the main environment of the planet.

The general process of formation of the earth's environment was through zoned melting in the **mantle**, situated around a nucleus. The dense and heaviest elements sank toward the center, increasing the size of the nucleus, and less dense and lighter elements rose to the surface, forming the **lithosphere**, the top-most part of which is the earth's crust.

By radiating heat into space, the earth's surface gradually cooled. The water vapors (gas) condensed, and became liquid water. Active elements and compounds, **discharged** by volcanic activity, interacted with the water, forming acids and salts. Deep **tectonic** processes and the composition of the earth's crust are **heterogeneous**.

Therefore, raised areas with thickened but chemically lighter crust have developed into land masses, and sunken areas with heavier crust have become the sea floor, covered by water. Oceanic crust is heavier, but thinner than continental crust, having a density of about 3 grams

■ Vocabulary

- atmosphere
- hydrosphere
- gravitational
- radioactive
- iron oxide
- nucleus
- mantle
- lithosphere
- discharge
- tectonic
- heterogeneous

per cubic centimeter and on average 7 kilometers thick, while continental crust has a density of about 3 grams per cubic centimeter and thickness between 10 and 70 kilometers. The process of plate tectonics has played a major role in the shaping of Earth's oceans and continents, as well as the life they harbor.

Vocabulary Check

✓ Choose the word that best completes each sentence. Change the form of the word if necessary.

1. The center of something may be called the __________.
2. __________ is also called rust.
3. We breathe the __________.
4. Something is __________ if it is not all the same.
5. The __________ is made of water.

Reading Comprehension

✓ Choose the best answer for each question.

1. The Earth was formed in __________.

   a. the explosion of a star
   b. a dust cloud
   c. the collision of asteroids
   d. a gravity well

2. The breakdown of radioactive elements released __________.

a. energy
b. tension
c. gravity
d. volcanoes

3. __________ sank and became the nucleus.

a. Rocks
b. Light elements
c. Dense elements
d. Water

4. The Earth's surface was cooled by __________.

a. radiating heat
b. water vapor
c. liquid water
d. volcanic activity

5. __________ became land masses.

a. Dry areas
b. Large areas
c. Areas with lighter crust
d. Areas with hills

6. According to the reading, what is 'gravitational forces'?

7. How similar is this explanation of the origin of the oceans to what you previously thought?

Did you know?

In the past 40 years, days have become longer. This is because so much water is dammed, and nearly all of it is north of the equator, that the weight of the entire planet has shifted. The good news is that you now get an extra four milli-seconds more sleep than your grandparents did.

The Five Oceans

Geologically, an ocean is an area of oceanic crust covered by water, while a continent is a large landmass identified as a tectonic plate resting on the crust. The oceanic crust is the thin layer of **solidified** volcanic **basalt** that covers the earth's mantle. It is thinner but denser than the continents.

The oceans occupy about 71% of the planet's surface and are conventionally divided into five oceans and smaller seas. They are fringed with coastlines that run for 360,000 kilometers, and their average depth is estimated about four kilometers. The word 'sea' is often interchangeably used with 'ocean', but strictly speaking, a sea is a body of **saline** water fully or partly **enclosed** by land.

Five major oceanic divisions are defined by the continents, various **archipelagos**, and other criteria. These divisions are in descending order:

- Pacific Ocean, which separates Asia and Australia from the Americas,
- Atlantic Ocean, which separates the Americas from Europe and Africa,
- Indian Ocean, which washes upon southern Asia and separates Africa and Australia,
- Southern Ocean, sometimes considered an extension of the Pacific, Atlantic and Indian Oceans, which **encircles** Antarctica,
- Arctic Ocean, sometimes considered a sea of the Atlantic, which covers much of the Arctic and washes upon northern North America and Eurasia.

For many years only four oceans were officially recognized, and then in the spring of 2000, the International

■ **Vocabulary**
- solidify
- basalt
- saline
- enclose
- archipelago
- encircle

Hydrographic Organization established the Southern Ocean and determined its limits.

Knowledge of the history of the formation of the earth permits us to understand the formation of useful minerals which have come to us from deep within the core of the earth. By tracing the different continents and oceans, geological structures and borders of lithosphere plates, scientists can reconstruct their previously adjoining areas, and predict the formation of petroleum and other exploitable minerals and **ores**. They can also try to predict **disastrous** earthquakes and other natural **hazardous** phenomena.

■ Vocabulary
- hydrographic
- ore
- disastrous
- hazardous

Vocabulary Check

✓ Choose the word that best completes each sentence. Change the form of the word if necessary.

1. __________ water contains salt.
2. A liquid will __________ when it becomes cold enough.
3. Metal is obtained from processing __________.
4. A group of islands is an __________.
5. You must be more careful in __________ areas.

Reading Comprehension

✓ Choose the best answer for each question.

1 The oceanic crust is made of __________.

a. hot lava
b. hot water
c. volcanic rock
d. sediment

2. The average depth of the oceans is __________.

a. one kilometer
b. four kilometers
c. five kilometers
d. ten kilometers

3. The Indian ocean is next to __________.

a. East Asia
b. South America & Antarctica
c. South America & Africa
d. Australia & Africa

4. The ocean around Antarctica is the __________.

   a. Pacific Ocean
   b. Atlantic Ocean
   c. Indian Ocean
   d. Southern Ocean

5. Studying __________ can help to find petroleum.

   a. plate borders
   b. national borders
   c. ocean currents
   d. volcanic currents

6. How much of the world's surface is covered by the oceans?

7. Which ocean or oceans do you think do not have the suitable name? And why?

Did you know?

Current sea level rise has occurred at a mean rate of 1.8 mm per year for the past century, and more recently, during the satellite era of sea level measurement, at rates estimated near 2.8 ± 0.4 [3] to 3.1 ± 0.7 mm per year (1993–2003). However from 2006 to 2010 sea level rise has dropped back levels approaching zero. (See the Satellite section). Current sea level rise is suggested to be due significantly to global warming, which will increase sea level over the coming century and longer periods. Increasing temperatures result in sea level rise by the thermal expansion of water and through the addition of water to the oceans from the melting of mountain glaciers, ice caps and ice sheets. At the end of the 20th century, thermal expansion and melting of land ice contributed roughly equally to sea level rise, while thermal expansion is expected to contribute more than half of the rise in the upcoming century.

Work Sheet

Water covers approximately 71% of the surface of the earth. It is conventionally divided into five oceans and smaller seas. We know the five oceans now. What about seas? Do you know how many seas exist on the planet, and what are some largest seas?

Unit 2

Ocean Life

Like on land, various species, in fact more than land species, live in the ocean. Most of the life in the ocean occurs in the warmer surface waters, so called Sunlight zone or Epipelagic zone, (0-200m). This unit aims to discover various forms of marine life and to understand environmental differences between marine and land life.

The assignment in this unit is to find out different species in the ocean as many as possible.

Manatees (sea cows)

Marine Habitats

A habit is an area where some particular species live. The oceans contain many habitats, which are broadly classified as coastal or open ocean.

Coastal habitats are in the region between the high tide mark and the edge of the continental shelf. Even though the shelf area is only seven percent of the ocean, most marine life is here. Since the shelf is usually less than 200 meters deep, there is enough sunlight for **photosynthesis**, and since it is close to land, there is a rich supply of **nutrients** from the land **runoff**.

Estuaries are where rivers meet the ocean in a partly enclosed area. Since the water in the ocean is calm, and it is close to the source of nutrients from land, estuaries are highly productive in marine life. This rich environment has always attracted human settlement. Over half of the world's population lives around estuaries.

The **intertidal** zone is the area that is alternately exposed and covered by the ocean tide. Within this region, there are rocky shores, sandy beaches, and mud flats. When the tide goes out, activity continues in the tide pools. On the rocks and under the sand or mud are many shellfish. The shore also attracts sea birds who make their nests and sea mammals who come to rest.

Under the water, **coral reefs** are among the richest ecosystems. Each reef is made by different types of coral growing together. As the reef grows, it becomes home to many kinds of **algae** and tropical fish. Most coral grows only in shallow water that is clear and warm.

If the water is too cold for coral, there are often **kelp**

■ Vocabulary
- photosynthesis
- nutrient
- runoff
- estuary
- intertidal
- coral reefs
- algae

beds. Kelp is a large, brown seaweed. It usually grows in water that is 2 to 30 meters deep. Kelp beds make an undersea forest that provides shelter and nutrients for many marine organisms.

The open ocean is less densely populated, because the water is poor in nutrients, but it is home to the marine animals that grow the largest, swim the fastest, dive the deepest, and migrate the farthest. The most plentiful organisms in the open ocean are the plankton, which are both plants (phytoplankton) and animals (zooplankton). They are eaten by small **forage** fish like **sardines**, which are then eaten by larger predator fish like tuna, and so on up the food chain.

- **Vocabulary**
  - kelp
  - forage
  - sardine
  - debris
  - hydrothermal vents

The deep sea lies below the reach of sunlight in the open ocean. For nutrition, life relies on organic **debris** such as waste and dead organisms that sink from above.

Far below, at an average depth of 2,100 meters, life on the sea floor clusters around **hydrothermal vents**, where volcanically heated water comes out of cracks. The water contains minerals, which feed bacteria, which then feed larger organisms. Each vent is like an island and may be home to unique species.

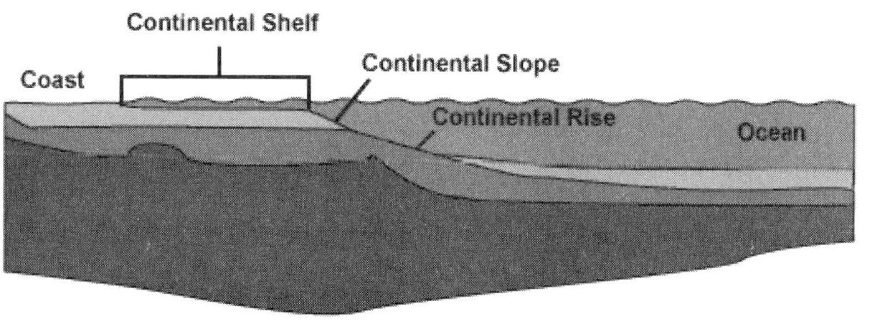

Vocabulary Check

✓ Choose the word that best completes each sentence. Change the form of the word if necessary.

1. We get __________ from food.
2. __________ areas are covered by water only part-time.
3. Rain water goes into the ground or into rivers as __________.
4. __________ are small fish.
5. __________ is a large type of seaweed.

Reading Comprehension

✓ Choose the best answer for each question.

1 All marine life needs __________.

a. sunlight
b. warm water
c. plankton
d. nutrients

2. Coral grows only in water that is warm, clear, and __________.

a. deep
b. shallow
c. nutritious
d. calm

3. Most marine life is in __________.

a. estuaries
b. deep sea
c. coastal shelves
d. intertidal zone

4. The largest marine animals live in the __________.

a. Pacific Ocean
b. Indian Ocean
c. coastal zone
d. open ocean

5. In the open ocean, the most plentiful life is __________.

a. plankton
b. seaweed
c. fish
d. whales

6. Which marine habitat has the least dense population of life?

7. Which marine habitat is most important for humanity?

Did you know?

The Great Barrier Reef in Australia is over 2, 300 kilometers long and is the largest thing on Earth made by living organisms. Due to human activity and environmental changes, the reef has lost over half of its coral since 1985.

Marine versus Land Mammals

Environmental differences and their impact on the creatures that live there

Living on land versus living in the ocean involves a lot more than simply being wet. Differences in the way we deal with simple things, such as keeping our bodies warm, finding food to eat, sleeping, and moving require very different solutions.

Gravity/Weight

On land, our bodies must be able to support the entirety of its own weight. This is not true of animals that live in the ocean. In water, the weight of the body is supported by the water. As such, marine mammals need fewer bones and can grow much larger without suffering any negative effects.

Temperature

On land, the temperature of the air can change fairly quickly. On sunny days, the weather can be quite warm, but get much cooler after dark. The temperature of the ocean changes much slower and remains fairly constant both day and night. In addition, mammals need to deal with the fact that water can **absorb** body heat many times faster than air can.

Presser/Density

Water and air both have weight which is something that most of us do not think about. Obviously water weighs more, and is denser, than air and as such, this weight (which we refer to as water pressure) and density must be dealt with by animals living in the sea.

> ■ **Vocabulary**
> - absorb
> - storage
> - blubber
> - insulator

Salinity/Salt

The ocean is full of salty water. Land mammals need fresh (un-salty) water to drink if they wish to stay alive. Marine mammals have had to adapt to a world where fresh water is not available, even though they need fresh water every bit as much as land animals.

Fat

Fat in most land animals including humans is generally not advantageous as it makes moving difficult because it is heavy. While some is necessary as an emergency **storage** of energy for use in case of **lean times**, it is generally not considered a benefit; hence most land mammals have relatively little body fat. Marine mammals on the other hand have a relatively large amount of body fat, which is called "**blubber**" and is beneficial for a number of different reasons.

First of all, fat is a very good **insulator** in water. Land mammals have hair to keep themselves warm since hair has the ability to trap air against the skin which is then heated, thus keeping the animal warm. It works well so long as

it stays dry. When hair gets wet, it loses its ability to trap air, and thus loses its ability to keep the skin insulated. This is why we get cold when we are wet. Fat, on the other hand, traps heat because it is a poor conductor of heat, meaning that heat does not move through fat very well, kind of like Styrofoam in cooler box.

> ■ **Vocabulary**
> • bladder
> • pressure
> • density

Secondly, fat floats. In the water, all animals need some way of floating. Fish typically have an organ called a "swim **bladder**" which is a gas filled sac that helps them float, but mammals do not have anything like that. To help them float, marine mammals use their fat. Since marine animals breathe air and need to be on the surface of the water to breathe, being able to float is important.

Size and weight

As many know, dolphins are relatively small, but some whale species can get to be very large. The Blue Whale, the largest animal that has ever lived, can grow to be 30 meters long and weigh up to 180 metric tons. They can grow this large because the ocean water supports their body weight easily and their skeletons do not have to support the weight as our skeleton does.

Food and water

Like us they need both food and water. And like us, they cannot drink sea water because it has too much salt in it. Drinking sea water would kill both humans and dolphins alike. We get our water from lakes and rivers, but where do dolphins get their water from? They get it from the fish they eat.

Vocabulary Check

✓ Choose the word that best completes each sentence. Change the form of the word if necessary.

1. Fat from marine mammals is called __________.
2. An __________ helps to keep you cool or warm.
3. Land mammals use fat just for energy __________.
4. Deeper under water, you feel more __________.
5. Something with less __________ than water will float.

Reading Comprehension

✓ Choose the best answer for each question.

1. Marin mammals get fresh water from __________.

a. rain	c. fish
b. runoff	d. seaweed

2. Compared to on land, temperature in the ocean __________.

a. is warmer	c. changes more
b. is colder	d. changes less

3. Marine mammals have __________ fat than land mammals.

a. more	c. lighter
b. less	d. denser

4. Land mammals need stronger __________ than marine mammals.

   a. fat
   b. skeletons
   c. hair
   d. muscles

5. Ocean water is __________ than the air.

   a. denser
   b. colder
   c. deeper
   d. cleaner

6. Why can marine mammals be larger than land mammals?

7. Besides they are warm-blooded, what do you think that mammals have characteristics that distinguish them from other sea life?

Did you know?

Pizza was very rare in America before 1945. It suddenly became popular after American soldiers returned from Italy after World War II. One of the most popular varieties at the time was anchovy pizza. Nowadays, the idea of anchovies on pizza polarizes Americans. Some love it, some won't even try it.

Work Sheet

Creatures in the ocean seem to be very different from those on land in many aspects, the differences being mostly made by their living environments. What are some biggest differences between them, and what are some common features among creatures in the ocean?

Unit 3

Maritime History

For different people and different time, the sea has served different things to humans. In this unit, you will discover when and for what purposes humans began diving into the sea, and how humans have exploited the sea.

The assignment in this unit is to research on any sea explorer who you are interested in or any piracy activity that you have heard or know.

Great Explorers

Travel on the surface of the ocean by the use of boats dates back to prehistoric times, but only in modern time extensive underwater **exploration** has become possible. Scientific investigations began with such early scientists as James Cook, Charles Darwin and Edmund Halley. Ocean exploration itself **coincided** with developments in shipbuilding, diving, navigation, exploration, and **cartography**.

Early exploration

4500 BC: Ocean diving begins

Around this time, coastal cultures like those in Greece and China began to dive into the sea as a source of food gathering, commerce, and possibly even warfare.

4000 BC: First sailing vessels

The ancient Egyptians developed sailing vessels, which were probably used only in the eastern **Mediterranean** and near the mouth of the Nile River.

600 BC: First sea routes

In search of **tin** and other resources, the ancient Phoenicians developed sea routes around the Mediterranean and into the Red Sea and Indian Ocean.

From Age of Exploration to Present

Hyecho (704-787) was a Silla Buddhist monk, who traveled from China to India in the years 723-727/728 CE.

■ Vocabulary
- exploration
  - explorer
- coincide
- cartography
- coastal
- Mediterranean
- tin

During his journey of India, Hyecho wrote a travelogue in Chinese named *Wang ocheonchukguk jeon* which means 'the memoir of the **pilgrimage** to the five kingdoms of India.' The journal is 28.5 centimeters in width and 358.6 centimeters in length and is the first overseas travelogue written by a Korean. It is regarded as one of the best historical travel journals as it provides information about political, cultural and economic customs of India and central Asia at that time. The five Indian kingdoms in the work refer to West, East, North, South and Central India.

Christopher Columbus (1492-1504) reached America looking for a sea route to the Indies, discovering various lands and islands and establishing a colony on Hispaniola. He called the inhabitants of the lands he visited '*indios*'(Spanish for "Indians")

James Cook (1768-1780) was a British explorer, navigator, cartographer, and captain in the Royal Navy. He explored the southern parts of the oceans looking for the southern continent. He was the first to use a marine **chronometer** to determine **longitude**.

- **Vocabulary**
- pilgrimage
- chronometer
- longitude

Charles Darwin (1809-1882) is best known for his contributions to evolutionary theory. He sailed on the Beagle, exploring the Galapagos and many other areas. It is this work which led him to develop the concepts of natural selection and evolution.

■ **Vocabulary**
- oceanographic
- decommission
- hull
- sea bed
- geophysical

First Oceanographic Research Vessel **(1882)**

The U.S. Fisheries Commission Steamer Albatross begins operations. The Albatross is the first vessel built by any government for the sole purpose of **oceanographic** research. This iron-**hulled** steamer would conduct serious marine research for nearly 40 years until it is finally **decommissioned** in 1921.

Deep-sea exploration is the investigation of physical, chemical, and biological conditions on the **sea bed** for scientific or commercial purposes. Deep-sea exploration is considered as a relatively recent human activity compared to the other areas of **geophysical** research, as the depths of the sea have been investigated only in comparatively recent years. The ocean depths still remain as a largely unexplored part of the planet and form a relatively undiscovered domain.

From http://www.seasky.org/

Vocabulary Check

✓ Choose the word that best completes each sentence. Change the form of the word if necessary.

1. The floor of the ocean is the __________.
2. East-West position is __________.
3. __________ is the making of maps.
4. A __________ city is next to the sea.
5. A __________ is a precise clock.

Reading Comprehension

✓ Choose the best answer for each question.

1 Six thousand years ago, Egyptians sailed in the __________.

a. North Sea
b. Indian Ocean
c. Atlantic Ocean
d. Mediterranean

2. Captain Cook was looking for ________.

a. Asia
b. South America
c. a southern continent
d. a route to India

3. Hyecho was a __________.

a. Chinese travelling to India
b. Chinese writing in Korean
c. Korean writing in Chinese
d. Korean writing about China

4. The first oceanographic research ship was built __________.

a. of wood
b. of metal
c. in England
d. in France

5. __________ exploration is the study of the ocean floor.

a. Maritime
b. Oceanographic
c. Scientific
d. Deep sea

6. Which explorer is famous for using a new navigation technique?

7. Which explorer contributed the most to scientific knowledge?

Did you know

Columbus thought he had reached Asia. It was Amerigo Vespucci who recognized that the Americas were not Asia. America is named after him.

Pirates

In many movies, a pirate's life is an exciting adventure. But what was life actually like for an 18th century pirate? And which parts of the movie pirate are real and which are invented?

A Pirate's Life

In reality, the average pirate was usually trying to **escape** from a difficult life. Some were ex-sailors who had **jumped ship**. Others were escaped slaves who wanted their freedom. They came from many different backgrounds. But on a pirate ship, equality was important. Men **elected** their captain and created the ship's rules together. They also fairly shared the income from their **plunder**.

Pirate Treasure

In popular culture, pirates are often shown with **chests** full of gold. It is true they took money from others. However, it was far more common for pirates to steal things like cloth, **spices**, and even medicine. Then they often sold these things. Of course, purchasing stolen goods from pirates was illegal, but many people did it. Also, unlike movie pirates, real pirates didn't bury their money. They blew it as soon as they could on women and **booze**. By reputation, pirates were rarely **sober**, even when sailing or fighting.

■ Vocabulary

- escape
- jump ship
- elect
- plunder
- treasure
- chest
- spice
- booze
- sober

Pirate Style

Movie pirates often wear eye patches and have wooden

legs. In reality, many pirates did look like this. Why? One factor was the poor living conditions. Life at sea was hard and dangerous. Disease was also common. For these reasons, some pirates lost eyes and legs. But many pirates did one thing for their health: they wore earrings just as in the movies. They believed putting weight on the ears stopped **seasickness**.

■ **Vocabulary**
- seasick

Report

Last night twelve pirates hijacked a cargo ship. The pirates say they will kill the crew and set fire to the ship if they don't get $3 million from the owners.

This morning an American warship caught the pirates' mother ship and arrested seven men on board. The US warship is now standing off from the hijacked cargo ship. The navy is ready to attack.

Vocabulary Check

✓ **Choose the word that best completes each sentence. Change the form of the word if necessary.**

1. To __________ someone is to chose a leader.
2. You must be __________ when driving a car.
3. Things you got by stealing is __________.
4. A __________ is used to store and carry things.
5. Even sailor can become __________ in rough weather.

Reading Comprehension

✓ Choose the best answer for each question.

1. What is the main idea of this reading?
   a. A pirate's life was dangerous but exciting.
   b. Some things we've heard or read about pirates are true, but others aren't.
   c. Modern-day pirates are similar to 18th century pirates.
   d. Modern stories about pirates are entirely wrong.

2. On many pirate ships, ____________________.
   a. men were like slaves
   b. there were several captains
   c. only ex-sailors were allowed
   d. the men shared the money they got

3. "They blew it." in the passage above means "They ________ the money."
   a. hid
   b. spent
   c. made
   d. saved

4. Which statement would David Moore probably agree with?
   a. Many pirates had a hard life and died young.
   b. The appearance of movie pirates is different from reality.
   c. A pirate's life was not as dangerous as we see in the movies.
   d. Many pirates were friendlier than we see in the movies.

5. Pirates believed wearing earrings ____________________.
   a. was fashionable
   b. stopped illness
   c. brought good luck
   d. was only for women

6. What kind of things did pirates usually steal?

7. How should we deal with piracy? Which statement below do you agree with? And why?

    1) Pirates should be punished by death. We should not arrest them, say, 'naughty, naughty,' and release them. We should sink their boats with all hands.

    2) Violence only makes more violence and killing pirates increases the risk for seafarers who are held hostage.

Did you know?

Around 1700, a French pirate was the first to use a black flag with a skull and crossbones, later known as the Jolly Roger.

Work Sheet

Since ancient times, the sea has been not only a rich food source for the people who gathered fish and shellfish along shores, but also served as shipping and trade route. What does the sea mean to you? Is that a place where we can gather food and resources, or enjoy marine sports?

Unit 4

Ships / Navigation

How much are you nautical? How much do you know about ships and navigation? Though we live nearby the ocean, thus seeing quite a lot of ships almost every day, we may not feel easy to answer to some questions like the above. The goal of this unit is to make you feel you have become a bit more nautical than before.

Talking about Ships

Learn the Difference between a Boat and a Ship.

To be **nautical**, you must learn the difference between a boat and a ship and use the correct term at all times! Generally speaking, ships are big and boats are small. A ship can carry a number of boats but no boat can carry a ship aboard. Ships are built for deep water use and are driven by sail or power. Most boats are not oceangoing vessels and some can be driven by **oars** as well as by sail or power.

Some exceptions: submarines are traditionally called boats (they used to be under 1,000 tons) and even oceangoing fishing vessels are usually still called fishing boats. Exception to the exception: **ballistic** missile submarines are ships of several thousand tons and are called ships. You will be **regarded as** quite nautical if you remember these facts!

Learn Port and Starboard.

The port side of a ship means the left side of it when facing forward. Notice that port and left both have four letters. Starboard **refers to** the right side. You can't be nautical until you know port from starboard. At night a vessel's port side shows a red light and its starboard side shows a green light. These lights can tell you which direction vessels are going at night if they are crossing your path.

▪ Vocabulary
- nautical
- oar
- ballistic
- regard as
- refer to

Learn Bow and Stern.

The bow is the front of the ship. When you take a bow you lean forward. The stern is the rear end of the boat or ship. When you take your bow your rear faces **aft**. Aft is toward the back or stern. These are important nautical terms.

> ■ Vocabulary
> • aft
> • deck
> • crucial

Learn Deck, Bulkhead, Overhead and Ladder.

There are no "floors" on vessels. Vessels have **decks** instead. Walls are called bulkheads and ceilings are called overheads. And stairs are called ladders aboard ships except for the staircases on passenger ships. Deck is a **crucial** nautical term for you to learn.

Types of ship

	**Bulk carrier** A bulk carrier, bulk freighter, or bulker is a merchant ship specially designed to transport unpackaged bulk cargo, such as grains, coal, ore, and cement in its cargo holds.
	**Tug Boat** A tugboat (tug) is a boat that maneuvers vessels by pushing or towing them. Tugs move vessels that either should not move themselves, such as ships in a crowded harbor or a narrow canal, or those that cannot move by themselves, such as barges, disabled ships, or oil platforms.

Container ship

Container ships are cargo ships that carry all of their load in truck-size intermodal containers, in a technique called containerization. They form a common means of commercial intermodal freight transport.

Oil tanker

An oil tanker, also known as a petroleum tanker, is a merchant ship designed for the bulk transport of oil. There are two basic types of oil tankers: the crude tanker and the product tanker

Chemical tanker

A chemical tanker is a type of tanker designed to transport chemicals in bulk. Ocean-going chemical tankers generally range from 5, 000 metric tons deadweight (DWT) to 40, 000 DWT in size, which is considerably smaller than the average size of other tanker types due to the specialized nature of their cargoes and the size restrictions of the port terminals where they call to load and discharge.

Cruise ship

A cruise ship or cruise liner is a passenger ship used for pleasure voyages, where the voyage itself and the ship's amenities are part of the experience, as well as the different destinations along the way.

LNG Carrier

An LNG carrier is a tank ship designed for transporting liquefied natural gas (LNG).

Warship

A battleship is a large armored war ship with a main battery consisting of heavy caliber guns. Battleships were larger, better armed and armored than cruisers and destroyers.

Vocabulary Check

✓ Choose the word that best completes each sentence. Change the form of the word if necessary.

1. The __________ is in the back of a ship.
2. A boat is moved by motor, sail, or __________.
3. The lower __________ of a ship are inside.
4. Water is __________ for life.
5. I __________ my captain as "Sir".

Reading Comprehension

✓ Choose the best answer for each question.

1. Which of the following is true?
   a. Starboard refers to the left side when facing forward.
   b. The stern is the front end of the ship.
   c. Floors on vessels are called decks.
   d. Steps on vessels are called stairs.

2. Submarines are called boats mainly because they _________.
   a. are not oceangoing vessels
   b. are small
   c. are built for deep water use
   d. do not use sail for power

3. A boat cannot _________.
   a. carry a ship
   b. go in deep water
   c. have a sail
   d. sink

4. Ships show a green light on starboard _________.
   a. in a harbor
   b. at sea
   c. when turning
   d. at night

5. Inside a ship, look up to see the _________.
   a. deck
   b. overhead
   c. bulkhead
   d. stern

6. What distinguish a ship from a boat?

7. What do you think ferry is a ship or a boat?

Did you know?

Some clocks and watches that use Roman numerals (I, II, III, etc.) use IV for 4 and some use IIII. Why?

Generally speaking, Roman numerals never have sequences of more than three instances of the same character, so IIII should be wrong. However, just as Korean culture has a superstition regarding the number 4 because it is homonymous with the word for death, so too did the Romans have a superstition. In their case, the spelling IV was the first two letters of the most powerful god, Jupiter (Iuppiter). Rather than risk his wrath, they often used the alternate spelling IIII.

Nautical Charts

In 2005, the American submarine USS San Francisco **collided** with an uncharted **seamount** about 675 km southeast of Guam. After an investigation, six crew members who were responsible for voyage planning **were disciplined** for not following proper navigation procedure.

Nautical charts summarize a huge amount of technical information. They are crowded with numbers and symbols for things like sea depth, currents, navigational aids, and underwater hazards such as rocks and **shipwrecks**. However, the information is often limited or **inaccurate**. For example, some of the San Francisco's charts indicated a potential hazard in the area, although they gave a location a few kilometers from the actual site of the seamount. The navigators had failed to be cautious in relying on their charts.

Part of the difficulty in making accurate charts is that the shape of the Earth is irregular. No system of specifying **latitude** and longitude will fit perfectly. Most existing nautical charts were based on a positioning system that does not match modern GPS positioning. The difference between the positions given by GPS and on a chart can be up to 100 meters in America and as much as 900 meters in eastern Asia.

The biggest problem, though, is that hydrographic surveys are expensive. Much of the ocean floor has not yet been precisely surveyed. Much existing survey data is from the 19th century, or even the 18th century for parts of the Pacific Ocean and Caribbean. At that time, measurement of latitude and longitude had **a large margin of error**, so surveyors focused on measuring the rel-

■ Vocabulary
- nautical chart
- collide
- seamount
- be disciplined
- shipwreck
- inaccurate
  ↔ accurate
- latitude

ative positions of observable landmarks. Navigators must always consider their position relative to charted features rather than just relying on GPS.

Today, hydrographic surveying is much more precise. In **critical** areas like harbors, position must be accurate to within 2 meters. In the open ocean, the required accuracy is 150 meters. It will be many years, though, before even the most critical areas are resurveyed to modern standards.

Meanwhile, paper charts are being replaced by electronic charts and GPS computers. This has led to dangerous situations. When navigators assume that the new systems are more accurate, they are tempted to go closer to danger areas. They forget that even though a chart is new, it might be based on survey data that is hundreds of years old.

- **Vocabulary**
- a large margin of error
- critical

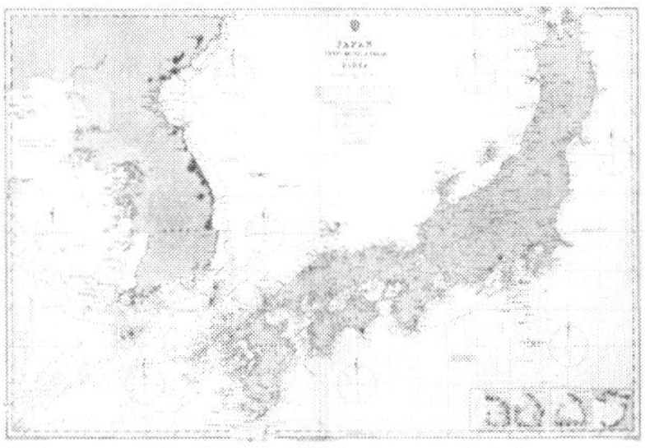

1873 British Nautical Chart of Japan and Korea

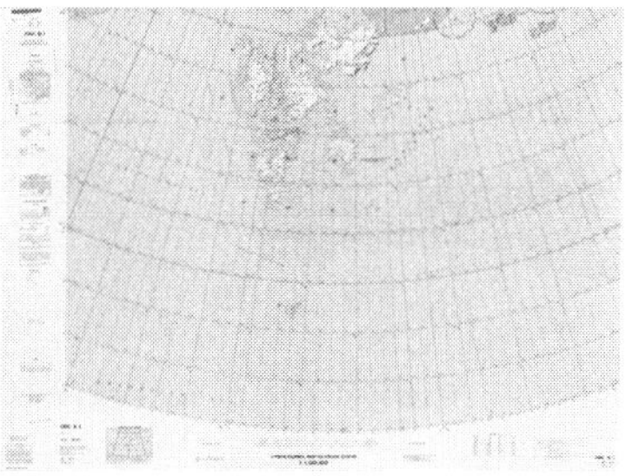

Operational Navigation Chart

See the YouTube, *Travel the Seas* at http://oceantoday.noaa.gov/traveltheseas/

Vocabulary Check

✓ Choose the word that best completes each sentence. Change the form of the word if necessary.

1. It is important that navigation is __________.
2. Ships may__________ are created by volcanoes.
3. __________ with something in shallow water.
4. Go north or south to change your __________.
5. Unless it is a submarine, a ship on the sea floor is a __________.

Reading Comprehension

✓ Choose the best answer for each question.

1. A nautical chart needs to show underwater __________.

   a. submarines　　c. fish
   b. pollution　　d. hazards

2. The San Francisco's navigators were not __________ enough.

   a. intelligent　　c. experienced
   b. careful　　d. educated

3. Charts of the Pacific Ocean may be up to __________ years old.

   a. 100　　c. 300
   b. 200　　d. 400

4. Modern hydrographic surveying is more __________.

a. precise
b. expensive
c. complete
d. difficult

5. It is dangerous to expect that GPS navigation is more __________.

a. expensive
b. affordable
c. accurate
d. popular

6. How is the round surface of the earth displayed on the flat surface of the chart?

7. Will electronic charts completely replace printed charts?

Reading for Fun

A British Navy ship and the Irish Coast guard had this conversation.

Irish: Please divert your course 15 degrees to the south, to avoid collision.

British: Recommend you divert your course 15 degrees to the north, to avoid collision.

Irish: Negative. You will have to divert your course 15 degrees to the south to avoid collision.

British: This is the Captain of a British Navy Ship. I say again, divert your course.

Irish: Negative. I say again, you will have to divert your course.

British: This is the largest ship in the British fleet. We are accompanied by 3 destroyers, 3 cruisers, and numerous support ships. I demand that you change your course 15 degrees to the north.

Irish: This is a lighthouse. Your call.

Resposibilities of officers onboard

1. Captain, master

The captain, or master, is ultimately responsible for all that goes on aboard the vessel. Usually he has not been integrated in the watch-keeping system on the bridge.

2. Chief officer (first mate)

The first mate is responsible for making up the stowage plan, supervision of loading and discharging of the cargo and general ship maintenance.

3. 2nd officer (second mate)

The second mate is responsible for the navigational equipment.

4. 3rd officer (third mate)

The third mate will often act as safety-officer. He or she is responsible for the maintenance of all the safety equipment on board.

The main duties of the Engineering officers in the engine-room department, are the maintenance and overhauling of the main engine and the auxiliary-engines.

5. Chief engineer

6. 1st engineer

7. 2nd engineer

8. 3rd engineer

9. Chief wireless operator

The tasks of the radio operator are to contact shore-based stations and other vessels in cases of distress, to transmit urgency messages, safety messages when there are imminent dangers to navigation, to listen to Notices to Mariners, weather reports and navigational warnings and to maintain contact with other ships for a safe and efficient voyage.

10. Boastswain

The boastswain, or bosun, is the head of the ratings.

Did you know?

The term "quartermaster" has two different uses. In the army, a quartermaster manages supplies. In the navy, they are responsible for navigation.

Work Sheet

From the earliest time, maritime navigation depended on the stars. What technological developments replaced navigation by the stars?

Unit 5

Ports and Port Management

Various activities, such as the movement of ships, containers, and other cargo, customs activities, occur at a port. The efficient management of a port involves managing these activities and resources. In this unit, you will have some idea what happens at a port and how it is managed.

Busan International Cruise Terminal

History of Ports

A port refers to a location on a coast or shore containing one or more harbors where ships can dock and transfer people or cargo to or from land. As of 2014, by continents, Europe has the vast number of port (3024), North America (2293) follows it, and then Asia (1720).There are 25 ports in South Korea.

Up to the 19th century, great ports **predominately** served as markets for international **staple** goods of value. Harbors were **integral** parts of the city, included in the urban **fortification** systems.

The second half of the 19th century through to the early 20th century was marked by increased industrialization and the expansion of city-ports. The ports changed from sites of trade to **nodes** of traffic and transport, channeling movement of cargo and flow of **migration**.

The city expanded with the port, and workers' neighborhoods developed rapidly, characterized by high population density, poor **dwelling** conditions and **casual** labor.

While the industrialization process was basically maintained until the mid-20th century, the face of the ports was changed by technological developments. Larger ships called for deep-water harbors outside of the old port areas. Modern ports were developed instead of the old inner-city ports, which were often **abandoned** or turned into tourist attractions. When containers were introduced in the late 1960s, this process increased even further, and many former port areas became urban **wastelands**.

■ Vocabulary

- predominately
- staple
- integral
- fortification
- node
- migration
- casual
- abandon
- dwell
- wasteland

In recent decades, international port cities have been increasingly affected by global transformation processes. Economic and technological changes have fundamentally restructured ports all over the world, dramatically altering the relation between port and city, the public image of cities, and the condition of people living and working around the ports. Until recently, harbors formed the core of urban development in all port cities.

From Port Cities as Areas of Transition: Comparative Ethnographic Research
by Waltraud Kokot

Vocabulary Check

✓ Choose the word that best completes each sentence. Change the form of the word if necessary.

1. Something __________ is not separate.
2. A __________ job does not have a regular schedule.
3. People usually do not return to something that they __________.
4. A __________ is where paths of travel meet.
5. People enter a __________ for protection.

Reading Comprehension

1 In history, ports were mainly __________.

a. international markets
b. fish markets
c. travel centers
d. construction centers

2. In modern times, ports became mainly __________.

a. construction centers
b. transport centers
c. more efficient
d. more crowded

3. Growing ports also caused workers' __________ to grow.

a. incomes
b. happiness
c. health
d. neighborhoods

4. Larger ships required ports with __________.

a. more workers
b. lower taxes
c. deeper water
d. newer equipment

5. Technological changes have __________ ports.

a. altered
b. preserved
c. isolated
d. reduced

6. Why were many ports in a city abandoned?

7. What is the best thing to do with an abandoned port?

Did you know?

From the beginning of the 15th century, the Korean government designated Busan as a trading port with the Japanese and allowed their settlement. Other Japanese settlements in Ulsan and Jinhae diminished later, but the Busan settlement, called Waegwan at the time, continued until Japan invaded Korea in 1592. The Japanese settlement, though relocated into Choryang later, continued to exist until Korea was exposed to modern diplomacy in 1876. In 1876, Busan became the first international port in Korea.

Port Authorities

A port is not just an area of land and water, it is also a collection of facilities and services to support the movement of ships and their cargo. A large port is a complex system and has many interactions with the surrounding community and environment. To manage all of this, governments create port authorities. In South Korea, the principle port is in Busan and the port's governing body is the Busan Port Authority.

A port authority is a public administration for a special-purpose district. Usually, it is governed by a board or **commission**, with members either appointed by the government or elected. Most port authorities are financially self-supporting. Instead of receiving tax money from the government, they cover their operating expenses by charging fees for the use of the port's facilities.

Commercial ports are expensive to build and maintain. Modern container ships keep getting bigger, requiring ports to keep updating their facilities to be larger and more efficient. A port authority must constantly assess the competitiveness of its waterways, docks, loading facilities, **warehouses**, **tugboats**, shipyards, and anything else. It may also manage facilities outside the port, such as airports, railroads, industrial parks, foreign-trade zones, and marine parks.

The port authority will directly manage official agencies for things like ship inspection, safety and environment, training and licensing, and security. It also contracts with companies to provide commercial services such as ship repair, **freight** warehousing, inland transport, customs processing, banking, and telecom- munications.

■ Vocabulary
- commission
- warehouse
- tugboat
- freight

Economic development is a major priority of a port

authority. It seeks to attract companies that will bring new services to the port. It educates local businesses on how to expand their operations. It promotes the port abroad to attract more traffic. **All the while**, it works with citizen groups and local government on **aesthetic** and environmental issues regarding use of the **waterfront**.

■ **Vocabulary**
- all the while
- aesthetic
- waterfront

Vocabulary Check

✓ Choose the word that best completes each sentence. Change the form of the word if necessary.

1. Container ships carry __________.
2. Beauty is a result of __________ qualities.
3. Things are kept in __________.
4. Boats are usually kept at the __________.
5. A __________ makes and enforces rules.

Reading Comprehension

1. Port authorities are created by __________.

   a. businesses
   b. ship companies
   c. citizen groups
   d. governments

2. "Self-supporting" in the passage above means that they do not get money from the __________.

   a. businesses
   b. ships
   c. government
   d. customers

3. Ports must grow because __________ keep growing.

   a. ships
   b. cities
   c. people
   d. oceans

4. A port authority will use another company to provide __________.

   a. security
   b. banking
   c. licensing
   d. ship inspection

5. Port authorities help the economy by __________ new companies.

   a. attracting
   b. starting
   c. promoting
   d. financing

6. What are the two main types of port authority?

7. What are the most important issues Busan Port Authority is facing today?

Did you know?

Container handling by the world's leading ports

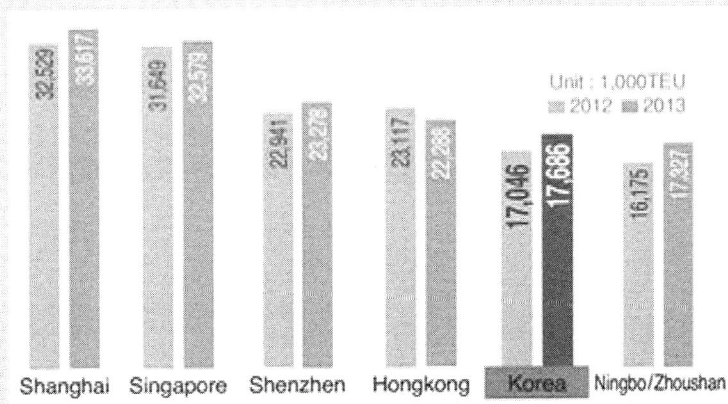

Work Sheet

Have you ever heard about Busan Port Authority (BPA)? The BPA is responsible for the overall development and growth of the port of Busan, which includes a number of facilities and terminals that handle a wide range of cargo transported in different forms, including containers as well as conventional and bulk cargo. Find out what type of port authority BPA is?

Unit 6

Maritime Law

Maritime law is a body of legal rules that governs ships, shipping, and crimes occurring on open water. In this unit, you will learn when and how the contemporary law of the sea immerged, and what the main purpose of the law is.

Law of the Sea

The oceans are a vast area, covering over 71% of the planet's surface. Have you ever wondered who controls them? What laws and rules apply to people while sailing on the oceans? Who makes the laws? Who **enforces** the laws? These are very important questions, and sometimes the answers can be difficult to find. Traditionally, the oceans were ruled by whoever was the strongest. The countries with the largest and most powerful navies controlled the oceans. This has changed very slowly. Over time most nations adopted the idea of "**territorial** waters," that is, nations began to claim that the waters near its coastlines were really an extension of that country's territory. These claimed waters usually extended out only a short distance from the land, usually only a couple of kilometers.

In those early days, the most important uses of a country's territorial waters were for the protection of its ports and for fishing, and as such, the short limits seemed to be enough. Today we use the oceans for many more things than just coastal fishing. Our ships are much larger and more powerful. In addition to fishing, we now search for **undersea** oil and mineral deposits. International trade and shipping has become very important, as has **pollution** control, environmental protection and scientific research.

In 1994 the countries of the world got together and wrote the United Nations Convention on the Law of the Sea. This became an international law that **laid out** the rules that would control how the oceans would be used and controlled. It was designed to be as fair as possible to all nations and yet still provide ways that coastal na-

▪ **Vocabulary**
- enforce
- territorial
  – territory
- undersea
- pollution
- lay out

tions could protect the waters near their shores.

Under this new law, most nations can claim an area of up to 200 miles from its shore which is called an "Exclusive Economic Zone" (EEZ) in which they have the **exclusive**, or sole, right to any economic uses of the zone, including fishing, oil drilling, or underwater **mining**. No company or person from any other country can do any of these activities in the EEZ without the owning nation's **permission**. However ships of all other nations are still allowed to travel through these zones for free so that international trade can continue.

■ **Vocabulary**
- exclusive
- mining
- permission

Vocabulary Check

✓ Choose the word that best completes each sentence. Change the form of the word if necessary.

1. __________ rights are not shared
2. A visa gives you __________ to enter a country.
3. Minerals and oil come from __________ the ocean floor.
4. __________ in the ocean kills much marine life.
5. The land and water claimed by a country is its ________

Reading Comprehension

✓ Choose the best answer for each question.

1 Historically, the oceans were ruled by __________.

a. kings
b. tradition
c. force
d. accident

2. Countries claimed territorial waters to protect their __________.

a. trade
b. fishing
c. water
d. navy

3. We now search the ocean for more __________.

a. pollution
b. coal
c. diamonds
d. oil

4. A country's EEZ gives it __________ economic rights.

a. primary
b. simple
c. sole
d. traditional

5. Foreign ships can freely __________ in an EEZ.

a. travel
b. fish
c. trade
d. mine

6. In any EEZ, what are foreign ships allowed to do without paying?

7. What are some of the things we do in the oceans today, other than fishing?

8. If some country claims much larger EEZ than 200 miles, then how should other countries respond?

Did you know?

The "High Seas" are the areas of the ocean beyond the control of any one nation and are legally owned by no single country. As a result, the law that applies depends on the nationality of the ship (or airplane) that the people are on.

Captain Goes down with the Ship

Captains Uncourageous: Abandoning ship long seen as a crime

Cowardice comes in many forms, but there's a special sense of shame reserved for captains who abandon ship.

South Korean authorities have arrested Capt. Lee Jun-Seok, who was one of the first to **flee from** the ferry Sewol as it sank on Wednesday, April 16, 2014. The incident came two years after Francesco Schettino, the captain of the **wrecked** cruise ship Costa Concordia, was charged with **manslaughter** and abandoning ship. The ship **ran aground** off the Italian coast in 2012, killing 32 people. Has the old idea that captains should not abandon ship itself been abandoned?

The Victorian notion that a captain should actually go down with the ship has become **archaic**. But his or her responsibility extends to executing the evacuation plan that all passenger ships are required to have and practice. It comes from the tradition that the captain has ultimate responsibility and should put the care of others ahead of his own well-being in the discharge of his duties.

In the middle of the 19th century, there were a number of incidents in which ships foundered and captains and their crews were either celebrated for leading the rescue or **reviled** for saving themselves while passengers drowned.

In the USA, the law indicates that a ship's master must be the last person to leave and make all reasonable efforts to save everyone and everything on it.

International standards for sea captains vary. Often, as in the case of Schettino, charges are brought based not on **dere-**

▪ Vocabulary
- cowardice
- flee from
- wreck
- manslaughter
- run aground
- archaic
- revile

liction of maritime duty but for **offenses** that might pertain on land as well, such as **negligence** and manslaughter. If the master is simply looking out for himself or herself, you have **breached** your duty both legally and morally, to your ship, your crew and your passengers. At sea, there is no question about who is in charge, so there is no doubt who is responsible for safety.

▪ **Vocabulary**
- dereliction
- offense
- negligence
- breach

From *National Public Radio*, April 18, 2014, Alan Greenblatt

Vocabulary Check

✓ Choose the word that best completes each sentence. Change the form of the word if necessary.

1. To kill someone by carelessness is __________.
2. People prefer to __________ danger.
3. People will usually __________ a bad person.
4. __________ is not doing what you should do.
5. __________ ideas are not modern.

Reading Comprehension

✓ Choose the best answer for each question.

1. The Costa Concordia sank __________ the Sewol.

   a. two years before
   b. one year before
   c. two months before
   d. two months after

2. Passenger ships are required to practice the __________ plan.

   a. turning
   b. loading
   c. travel
   d. evacuation

3. In the 1800s, captains were __________ for staying on sinking ships.

   a. stupid
   b. famous
   c. praised
   d. criticized

4. In America, a ship captain must leave the ship __________.

   a. when it sinks
   b. after all passengers
   c. to help passengers
   d. in a lifeboat

5. Captain Schettino was charged with __________.

   a. cowardice
   b. manslaughter
   c. murder
   d. theft

6. What was the responsibility that the Capt. of Sewol and Capt. of Costa Concordia did not fulfill?

7. Why do people think a captain has the responsibility of going down with the ship? Is there any other situation that you think the leader has the same responsibility?

Did you know?

The Morse code sequence SOS (•••---•••) was the standard maritime radio distress signal from 1908 until 1999. When radio voice communication became common in the 1920s, "Mayday" was introduced as the spoken equivalent of SOS.

May day: Great danger, help me!
Pan-pan: I've got a problem, stand by!

Work Sheet

A country has the exclusive right to any economic uses of the EEZ, including fishing, oil drilling, or underwater mining. This zone extends up to 200 miles from the country's shore. Do you know how 200 miles was set up?

Unit 7

Navy / Coast Guard

Both the Navy and the Coast Guard are branches of armed forces. Then, what makes them different from one another? In this unit, you will have a chance to think about the differences between Navy and Coast Guard, and why some countries have the Coast Guard even though they have the Navy.

Battle of Myeongnyang

In 2014, an astonishing incident happened at the South Korean box office. The historic **epic** film, *The Admiral: Roaring Current* (Myeongnyang in Korean) became the highest **grossing** film **of all time** in South Korea, with more than 17 million admissions, the first **home-grown** film to gross over USD 100 million. Do you happen to be one of viewers?

The movie depicted the battle of Myeongnyang, which took place during the Japanese invasions of Korea (then-named 'Joseon') from 1592 to 1597. This battle is regarded as one of the most remarkable victories in world naval history. The Joseon kingdom's navy, led by Admiral Yi Sun-sin, awell-respected Korean naval commander, fought the Japanese navy in the Myeongnyang **Strait**,* off the southwest of the Korean peninsula on October 26, 1597.

Admiral Yi had studied several locations and decided to **lure** the Japanese navy into the Myeongnyang Strait. This stretch of water is known for its powerful tidal current that changes direction every three hours. The Japanese entered the strait when the tide was favorable to them. When the current reversed, the Japanese ships began to **drift** backwards and collide with each other, causing damage. In the confusion, Admiral Yi ordered his ships to advance and press the attack, **plunging** into 30 Japanese ships. The dense formation of Japanese ships crowded in the narrow strait made a perfect target for Joseon cannon fire. The strong tides prevented those in the water from swimming to

■ Vocabulary
- epic
- gross
- of all time
- home–grown
- strait
- lure
- drift
- plunge

* The word 'Myeongnyang' was from Chinese characters. It is also called Uldolmok which is a pure Korean name, meaning a strait where rocks cry.

shore, and most Japanese sailors who abandoned sinking or damaged ships drowned. By the end of the battle, the Japanese had lost 31 warships. In this battle, Admiral Yi defeated a fleet of 133 Japanese warships with just 13 warships, thanks to his clever tactics that lured the enemy into the strait's hazardous tides.

■ **Vocabulary**
- extraordinary

The battle of Noryang (December 16, 1598), fought in the straits that divide Namhae Island from the mainland, was the last battle of the Japanese invasion. At the height of the battle, Yi Sun-sin was hit by a bullet and died in the command tower of his ship as news was brought to him of his victory.

This heroic patriot has been greatly admired both at home and abroad, due to mainly his tactical brilliance. Military historians have placed him alongside such great captains as Horatio Nelson. Interestingly, one of his greatest admirers was Japanese admiral Togo Heihachiro. After defeating the Russian fleet at Tsushima in 1905, Heihachiro said, "You may compare me to Nelson, but not to Yi Sun-sin: He is too **extraordinary** for anyone."

Vocabulary Check

✓ Choose the word that best completes each sentence. Change the form of the word if necessary.

1. A ship will just __________ without power.
2. A __________ is a narrow area of sea between two land areas.
3. An __________ story is not short or simple.
4. Something __________ is not imported.

5. Your __________ salary is before taxes and expenses.

Reading Comprehension

✓ Choose the best answer for each question.

1 Yi Sun-sin chose Myeongnyang for the battle because __________.

a. it was close to his port

b. it had currents that changed direction

c. it had a lot of room for moving

d. it had shallow water

2. At Myeongnyang, most Japanese died from __________.

a. arrows

b. cannon

c. fire

d. drowning

3. Yi Sun-sin's final battle was at __________.

a. Busan

b. Ulsan

c. Myeongnyang

d. Noryang

4. Yi Sun-sin was killed by a __________.

a. spear

b. fire

c. bullet

d. arrow

5. The Japanese defeated the Russians at __________.

a. Tsushima

b. Tokushima

c. Namhae

d. Vladivostok

6. Where was Admiral Yi's last battle?

7. What do you think was the chief reason for the movie, Myeongnyang's box office hit?

Did you know?

Yi Sun-sin wrote in his report to King Sonjo: "Previously, foreseeing the Japanese invasion, I had a turtle ship made. With a dragon's head, from whose mouth we could fire our cannons, and with iron spikes on its back to pierce the enemy's feet when they tried to board. Because it is in the shape of a turtle, our men can look out from inside, but the enemy cannot look in from outside. It moves so swiftly that it can plunge into the midst of even many hundreds of enemy vessels in any weather to attack them with cannon balls and fire throwers."

Coast Guard

As part of a nation's responsibility to **regulate** and control activities within its Exclusive Economic Zone (EEZ), it must set up a search and rescue service to assist people who get lost at sea or are in danger. The most common type of service is the coast guard service. A nation's coast guard **is charged with** the responsibility of patrolling the waters of its nation's EEZ and rendering aid to any boats, ships, airplanes, or people who require assistance. In addition, they are also called upon to enforce maritime law, protect the marine environment, and to maintain the river, intracoastal and **offshore** aids to navigation. In many countries, they are also responsible for operating harbors, ports and lighthouses.

The United States Coast Guard is one such organization. Founded in the late 1700s, the U.S. Coast Guard has been saving lives and protecting ships in and around the United States since its beginning. Though originally formed as the Revenue Cutter Service for the **purpose** of regulating foreign imports into the U.S., it quickly grew into the search and rescue service we know today.

In addition to saving lives, the U.S. Coast Guard is also expected to prevent other countries from **engaging** in illegal fishing, **smuggling** of drugs or people, piracy, and to organize and control oil spills and other shipping **disasters** and to promote environmental conservation. To perform these tasks the coast guard units typically use ships, high speed boats, airplanes and helicopters.

Today most nations have a coast guard service of their own, and many are very similar to the United States' coast guard service. They are modern, highly trained, highly

■ **Vocabulary**
- regulate
- be charged with
- offshore
- purpose
- engage
- smuggling
- disaster

motivated, and use the latest computer, radio, and satellite communications equipment to perform their duties and have saved hundreds of lives around the world. Those of us who will travel out to sea, by ship or airplane, can take comfort in the fact that if we get into trouble the coast guard will be there to help us.

USCG (US Coast Guard)		**KCG (Korean Coast Guard)**	
	E-1 Seaman recruit (장정)		
	E-2 Seaman Apprentie (이병)		Auxiliary Policemen (의경)
	E-3 Seaman (일병)		
	E-4 Petty Officer 3rd Class (상병)		Policeman (순경)
	E-5 Petty Officer 2nd Class (병장)	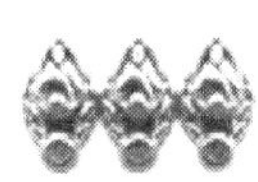	Senior Policeman (경장)
	E-6 Petty Officer 1st Class (사하)		Assistant inspector (경사)
	O-2 Lieutenant Junior Grade (중위)		Inspector (경위)
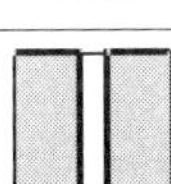	O-3 Lieutenant (대위)		Senior Inspector (경감)

	O-5 Commander (중령)		Superintendent (경정)
	O-6 Captain (선장)		Senior Superintendent (총경)
	O-7 Real Admiral-lower half (후면제독-절반 하위)		Superintendent General (경무관)
	O-8 Real Admiral-upper half (후면제독-절반 상위)		Senior Superintendent General (치안감)
	O-9 Vice Admiral (담당제독)		Chief Superintendent General (치안정감)
	O-10 Commandant of the CG (CG의 사령관)		Commissioner General (치안총감)

Vocabulary Check

✓ Choose the word that best completes each sentence. Change the form of the word if necessary.

1. A tsunami is one of the biggest maritime __________.
2. The main __________ of the Coast Guard is to protect.
3. People try to __________ illegal things into a country.
4. A criminal will be __________ a crime.
5. A navigation light can be on land or __________.

Reading Comprehension

✓ Choose the best answer for each question.

1. A coast guard patrols a country's __________.

 a. rivers
 b. lakes
 c. EEZ
 d. ports

2. A coast guard does not help __________.

 a. sinking ferries
 b. lost fishermen
 c. travel agents
 d. drowning swimmers

3. The US Coast Guard was created to regulate __________.

 a. fishing
 b. imports
 c. pirates
 d. travel

4. A coast guard does not help prevent __________.

 a. smuggling
 b. oil spills
 c. tourism
 d. accidents

5. A coast guard does not help look for lost __________.

 a. ships
 b. swimmers
 c. airplanes
 d. trains

6. What was the U.S. Coast Guard originally formed for?

7. Should the Coast Guard be distinct from the Navy?

Vessel: May-day, May-day, May-day. This is Alpha Papa three nine. Alpha Papa three nine. Alpha Papa three nine. May-day. Our position is: five-five degrees north, zero-four degrees east. Our vessel is sinking. We require immediate rescue. We have nine persons onboard. We are taking a lifeboat. Over.

Coastguard: May-day Alpha Papa three nine. This is Hotel Lima Charlie one zero five. Received your May-day. Over.

Did you know?

The United States Coast Guard's Rescue Swimmer program is considered by many to be one of the longest and most difficult professional training programs in the world.

The difference between Navy and Coast Guard in the case of the U.S.

The Navy is a warfighting force governed by title ten of the U.S. Code and is part of the department of defense. The mission of the U.S. Navy is to maintain, train, and equip combat-ready Naval forces capable of winning wars, deterring aggression and maintaining freedom of the seas. The Coast Guard is a maritime law enforcement and search and rescue entity governed by title 14 of U.S. code and is part of the department of homeland security.

http://www.quora.com/What-is-the-difference-between-the-US-Coast-Guard-and-US-Navy

Work Sheet

The Korean Coast Guard underwent some structural changes after the Sewol tragedy on April 16, 2014. How did the KCG change? What's your opinion about th change?

Unit 8

Fisheries / Fishing

Korea as a peninsula country has vast territorial waters. Due to this geographical accessibility of sea, fisheries have made a significant contribution to the development of the nation. In this unit, you will learn different types of fisheries and their features. You will also see how food chain works at sea.

Jagalchi Market

Aquaculture

Fish have played an important role throughout the history of humanity. Today, fish are the basis of a major industry around the globe. The modern fishery comes in many varieties.

One type is called wild fisheries or capture fisheries. They are usually found in the seas of oceans, but some are found in land, in rivers and lakes. Most of them are to be found in shallow water above a **coastal shelf**. A coastal shelf is the edge of a continental land mass that is **submerged** in the ocean. Because of the oceanographic phenomenon of **upwelling**, where winds drive the cooler and more nutrient-rich waters, coastal shelves tend to be more densely populated with fish.

The other type is fish farming. Similar to regular farming, the fish are grown in a controlled environment, such as ponds, tanks, and other enclosures. Fish farming accounts for 21% of the total fishery industry in South Korea. This is sometimes known as **aquaculture**. The term aqua is the Latin word for water, while culture refers to something that is cultivated.

Despite the name, fishery does not include only fish. Aquatic plants are also gathered or cultivated and **subsequently** sold. While many cultures throughout the world eat fish, the ocean's plants are eaten by far fewer. Only

■ Vocabulary
- constitute
- coastal shelf
- submerge
- upwelling
- aquaculture
- subsequently

six countries (Chile, China, Indonesia, Japan, South Korea and the Philippines) have 65% of the world's capture fisheries of aquatic plants. As opposed to the marketing of fish, the cultivation of aquatic plants by farming in South Korea is almost 98% farmed rather than wild. In North Korea, on the other hand, it is 100%.

■ Vocabulary
- fueled by

Fish will continue to be a part of human diet although they are no longer considered the healthy food choice they once were. (The healthy oils they give actually come from the plants they eat, which we can get directly by eating the plants ourselves.) But fisheries are a stable industry, **fueled by** a constant demand for their supply.

Vocabulary Check

✓ Choose the word that best completes each sentence. Change the form of the word if necessary.

1. Water on the __________ is not very deep.
2. Growing land plants and animals is not part of __________.
3. To __________ is to go under the water.
4. __________ water comes from below.
5. I graduated and __________ got a job.

Reading Comprehension

✓ Choose the best answer for each question.

1 Wild fisheries are not found in __________.

a. oceans
c. clouds
b. lakes
d. rivers

2. Most capture fisheries are located in __________.

a. costal shelves
c. deep water
b. warm water
d. harbors

3. Aquaculture is the __________ of fish.

a. capturing
c. eating
b. releasing
d. growing

4. __________ seaweed in North Korea comes from farms.

a. No
c. Most
b. Some
d. All

5. The healthy oils in fish meat come from __________.

a. plankton
c. exercise
b. plants
d. salt water

6. What is the difference between South and North Korea in aquiculture?

7. Why are captured fisheries of aquatic plants mostly in Asia?

Did you know?

The Germanic people did not create the word fish. It comes from the Latin word piscis. Many Romantic words (i.e., words from languages that can be traced back to Rome) that begin with the *p* sound were changed to an *f* sound as the speakers moved in to the Bavarian lands. Another example is pater which eventually became father in English. However, we still use the *p* sound in the word paternal.

Food Chain at Sea

The aquatic ecosystem is composed of many species of fish. In **the survival of the fittest**, whole species of fish have come and gone throughout the history of the oceans. A **fragile** and constantly changing ratio of each species to the others has existed at every point in history. Overfishing occurs when humans disrupt this delicate balance by **extracting from** the waters too many of a certain species.

The problem of overfishing is not simply a matter of a species being unavailable until it repopulates. Even if enough fish are left, the damage done by overfishing could result in other species growing too strong. For example, if enough **trout** are removed, the local **carp** may grow too numerous, leaving the trout unable to sustain their reproductive capacity. In other words, humans did not kill them, but they weakened them enough that their natural **predators** can.

Humans are not always the **instigator** in **the chain of circumstances**. In 1971, Peru sold 10,200,000 metric tons of **anchovies**, but the following year, El Niño weather conditions killed so many anchovies that Peruvian fisheries could only get four metric tons of the species, but even this tiny amount prevented the local anchovy population from regaining its reproductive capacity for several years.

Humans are often **portrayed** as an unnatural predator, destroying species of fish for no other reason than making profit. Without denying this, it is also true that humanity is the only being in the history of the planet to concern itself with the preservation of other, **endangered**

■ Vocabulary
- the survival of the fittest
- fragile
- extract from
- trout
- carp
- predator
- instigator
- the chain of circumstances
- anchovy
- portray
- endanger
- to this end

species. **To this end**, there are protests and organizations dedicated to raising awareness of these animals. Here's a question to ponder: if it is wrong for humans to kill off an entire species of fish, would it also be wrong for a species of whale to kill off that species of fish as well? Is humanity's quest for profit less valid than the whales' quest for survival?

Kinds of fish

	**Anchovy** It is common in the Pacific Ocean south from the Sea of Okhotsk, widespread in the Sea of Japan, Yellow Sea, and East China Sea, and near the coasts of Japan. They live up to 2–3 years.
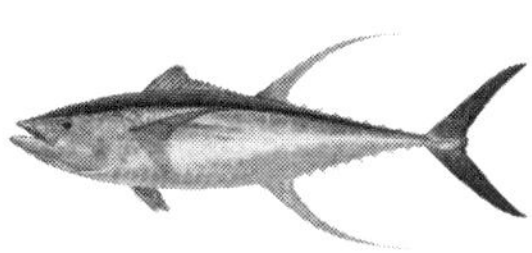	**Tuna** A tuna is a saltwater fin fish that belongs to the tribe Thunnini. Their circulatory and respiratory systems are unique among fish, enabling them to maintain a body temperature higher than that of the surrounding water.
	**Salmon** The salmon is native to tributaries of the North Atlantic and Pacific Ocean. Salmon are intensively produced in aquaculture in many parts of the world.
	**Carp** The carp is a medium-sized member of the common carp family Cyprinidae. It occurs widely in northern European regions.

Scallop

They are a cosmopolitan family of bivalves, found inall of the world's oceans, though never in freshwater. They are one of very few groups of bivalves to be primarily free-living.

Mackerel

Mackerel typically have vertical stripes on their backs and deeply forked tails. Many species are restricted in their distribution ranges, and live in separate populations or fish stocks based on geography.

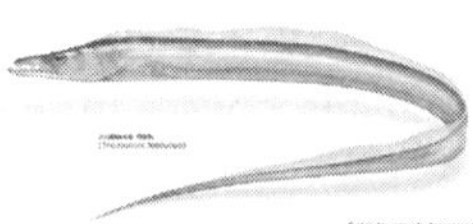

Cutlassfish

Fish of this family are long, slender, and generally steely blue or silver in color, giving rise to their name. They have reduced or absent pelvic and caudal fins, giving them an eel-like appearance, and large fang-like teeth.

Shark

Sharks are a group of fish characterized by a cartilaginous skeleton, five to seven gill slits on the sides of the head, and pectoral fins that are not fused to the head.

Monk fish

The sea monk (also monk-fish or monkfish) is a sea creature found off the eastern coast of the Danish island of Zealand. It have a lot of vitamin A.

Cod

Cod is the common name for the genus Gadus of demersalfishes, belonging to the family Gadidae.

Herring

Herrings often move in large schools around fishing banks and near the coast. The most abundant and commercially important species belong to the genus Clupea, found particularly in shallow

Abalone

Abalone is a common name for any of a group of small to very large edible sea snails, marine gastropod mollusks in the family Haliotidae.

Oyster

Oyster is used as a common name for a number of different families of saltwater clams, bivalve mollusks that live in marine or brackish habitats.

Flounder

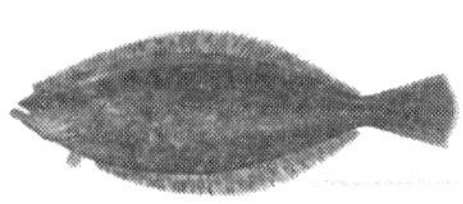

Flounder are a group of flatfish species. They are demersal fish found at the bottom of oceans around the world; some species will also enter estuaries.

Crab

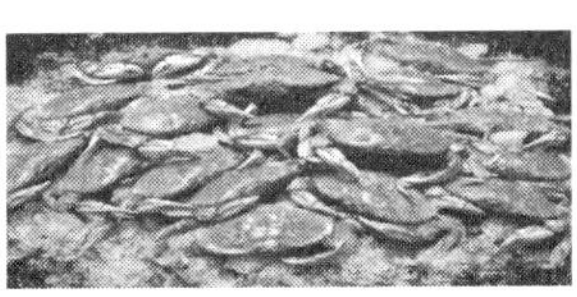

They live in all the world's oceans, in fresh water, and on land, are generally covered with a thick exoskeleton and have a single pair of claws. Many other animals with similar names

Shrimp

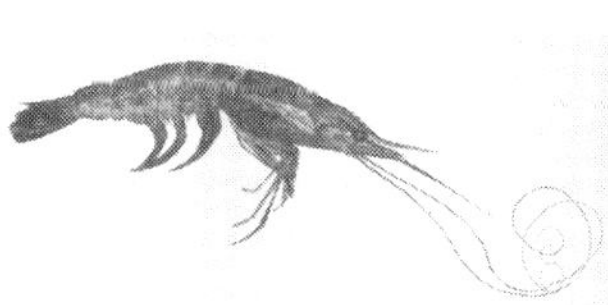

Shrimp are widespread and abundant. They can be found feeding near the seafloor on most coasts and estuaries, as well as in rivers and lakes. To escape predators, some species flip off the seafloor and dive into the sediment.

<table>
<tr><td>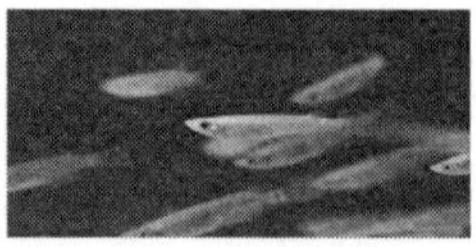</td><td>Ricefish
The ricefishes are a family of small ray-finned fish that are found in fresh and brackish waters from India to Japan</td></tr>
<tr><td></td><td>Eel
An eel is any fish belonging to the order Anguilliformes, which consists of four suborders, 20 families, 111 genera and about 800 species. Most eels are predators.</td></tr>
<tr><td></td><td>Catfish
Catfishes are a diverse group of ray-finned fish. Named for their prominent barbels, which resemble a cat's whiskers, catfish range in size and behavior from the heaviest and longest.</td></tr>
</table>

Vocabulary Check

✓ Choose the word that best completes each sentence. Change the form of the word if necessary.

1. Traditional gardens may have __________ in the water.
2. An __________ will begin something.
3. Something __________ is easy to break.
4. A __________ eats other animals.
5. Pollution can __________ marine life.

Reading Comprehension

✓ Choose the best answer for each question.

1. Species of fish survive if they are the __________.

   a. largest
   b. fastest
   c. fittest
   d. smartest

2. Overfishing can cause __________.

   a. pollution
   b. species imbalance
   c. high prices
   d. trade imbalance

3. If too many fish are caught, they are unable to __________.

   a. compete
   b. migrate
   c. reproduce
   d. swim

4. After El Nino, Peru's __________ population was reduced.

   a. squid
   b. tuna
   c. anchovy
   d. shark

5. Protesters want to protect __________ species of fish

   a. popular
   b. delicious
   c. endangered
   d. fittest

6. The third paragraph mentions a 'chain of events.' What is the chain of events in the second paragraph?

7. Humans are said to be the only species on the planet without a natural predator. Do you agree or disagree? Why or why not?

Did you know?

There is disagreement about this. Conservative writers say that the noun, fishes, is always wrong, but others find it acceptable when talking about many different species of fish. However, a sentence like 'We ate three fishes last night' would always be considered incorrect.

Work Sheet

Korea is a peninsula surrounded by water on three sides. Due to this geographic location, many Korean lives have been deeply related to the sea. Does your life happen to be related to the sea somehow in some way? Do you know anyone whose life relies on the sea? Tell us about it.

Unit 9

Sea Commerce

With the development of technology, traditional maritime activities have changed rapidly operating megaports, massive megaton tankers, gigantic passenger liners, and so forth. In this unit, you will learn maritime commerce that has gone beyond traditional maritime activities.

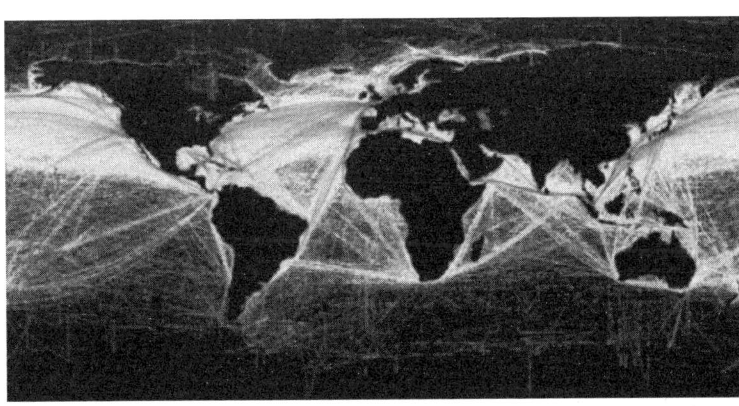

Shipping routes

Container Ships

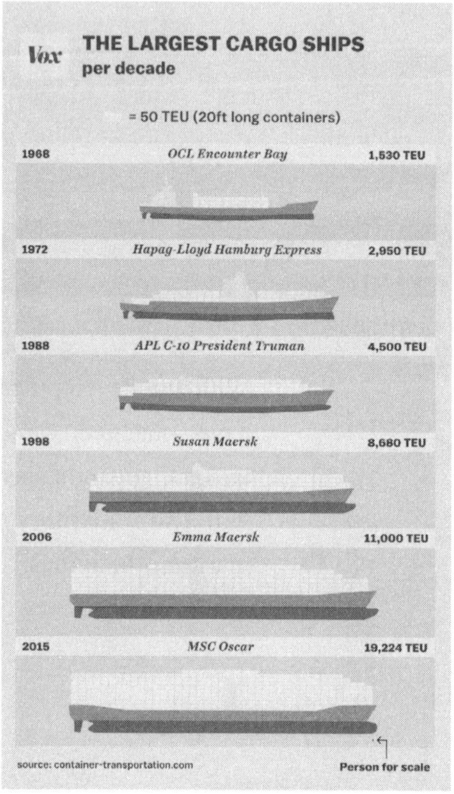

Maritime commerce has been an increasingly important component of the global economy. Modern maritime commerce is generally defined by large, **containerized** shipping moving through megaports, which form the **backbone** of just-in-time international trade.

The **advent** of modern maritime commerce began in 1956 when an American trucking company executive named Malcolm McLean designed a box, that we now call a "shipping container." These simple boxes, known in the industry as" intermodal **freight** containers," and the ships designed to carry them, have changed the world forever.

What made these boxes so special was that, since they were of a standard size, they could easily be moved by and between a large number of shippers. These boxes are typically 20-feet (6.1 m) or 40-feet (12.19 m) long and about 8-feet (2.44 m) high by 8-feet (2.44 m) wide. They are made of steel and have heavy wood floors. Since they were designed to be **reusable** and last a very long time, they are fairly inexpensive to use.

■ Vocabulary
- containerize
- backbone
- advent
- freight
- reusable

Packed at the factory, the box is **sealed** and loaded onto a truck, taken to either a **rail yard** and put on a train, or directly to a port and loaded on a ship. The box is not opened or unpacked again until it arrives at the customer's place of business.

■ Vocabulary
- seal
- rail yard
- equation
- rail yard
- add up

As amazingly simple as the box itself is, the other half of the **equation** is the development of the container ships. Modern container ships are specifically designed to carry as many of these boxes as possible, thus reducing the overall cost of moving each box. The very first container ships carried a mere 58 boxes, but today many modern ships can carry as many as 10,000 boxes in one trip. This can **add up** to very significant savings for the individual shipper.

Ship size has continued to grow over the years. Many of the larger container ships are too big to pass through the Panama Canal, and if they keep growing, they may get so big that they won't be able to fit through the Suez Canal either! Where will all this growth end? No one knows for sure, but in 2008 South Korean shipbuilder STX announced plans to construct a container ship capable of carrying 22,000 containers, and with a proposed length of 450 meters and a width of 60 meters. If constructed, the container ship would become the largest seagoing vessel in the world.

Vocabulary Check

✓ Choose the word that best completes each sentence. Change the form of the word if necessary.

1. Voting is the __________ of democratic government.
2. Ships usually carry people or __________.
3. Trains are loaded at a __________.
4. A __________ container saves money.
5. An envelope is __________ to protect the contents.

Reading Comprehension

✓ Choose the best answer for each question.

1 Shipping containers were first designed for __________ use.

a. storage
b. railroad
c. truck
d. maritime

2. Shipping containers are made mostly of __________.

a. aluminum
b. steel
c. iron
d. wood

3. After it is sealed, a container is opened only by the __________.

a. customer
b. customs agent
c. transporter
d. dock workers

4. Large container ships make transport __________.

   a. faster　　　　c. cheaper
   b. cleaner　　　d. harder

5. Container ships may become too __________ to be used everywhere.

   a. many　　　　c. old
   b. expensive　　d. big

6. What are benefits of shipping containers?

7. What are economic effects of having bigger ships?

Did you know?

The largest modern container ship, MSC Oscar was launched January 8, 2015. Oscar, built by Daewoo Shipbuilding & Marin Engineering, is 395.4m long and 59m wide. In other words, the deck of Oscar is nearly four football fields laid end to end. It can carry more than 19,000 shipping containers.

Shipping and the Economy

International trade has grown at such a rapid rate that it has caused the **fusion** of many industries with traditional maritime activities. There are now many maritime activities besides the traditional ones of military, fishing, and cargo shipping.

In today's modern world, a great number of support services such as ship financing, marine insurance, maritime legal services, maritime education and research & development have also shown huge growth. With the spread of international trade, international travel has also grown quickly.

Speaking of international trade, the importance of modern shipping cannot be ignored. Nearly every item we use every day, from our computers, to our shoes, to the food we have for lunch all moved, **at one point or another**, on board a ship. According to reports, nearly 90% of world trade is transported by sea. The reasons for this **terrific** growth in international trade can be traced to a few modern developments, namely, advances in communications, computers, and containerized shipping and ships.

The improvements in shipping have also changed the focus of world business. With the advent of cheaper shipping costs, many countries that have less expensive labor costs, mostly in Asia, have been able to attract more and more businesses to their countries. As a result, 14 of the world's 20 busiest ports are now in Asia and handle over one third of the entire world's shipping containers.

These changes have also affected related businesses too. In 2004 Korea became the world's largest ship builder, with most ships being built in the port cities of Busan

■ Vocabulary
- fusion
- at one point or another
- terrific

and Ulsan. Of the Korean shipbuilding companies, the largest is Hyundai Heavy Industries (HHI), and is Korea's largest user of steel. Other shipbuilders include Daewoo, Samsung and Hanjin.

■ **Vocabulary**
- expand
- contribute to

In addition to shipping and shipbuilding, the use of ports and other related facilities has **contributed to** huge increases in other areas of economic growth. While it might be easy to think of only the port as "maritime," we have to realize that many, if not most, of the people and businesses in such a city support, or are supported by, the activities of the port. Banks, restaurants, fuel, and all other businesses are directly or indirectly affected by the port activities.

Jobs related to ships

1. **Shipbrokers** are specialists (i.e. brokers) who intermediate/negotiate between shipowners and charterers who use ships to transport cargo, or between buyers and sellers of vessels.

2. An **insurance broker** (also **insurance agent**) sells, solicits, or negotiates insurance for compensation.

3. **Marine officers** (해기사) are licensed professional seafarers who work in either the deck or engine departments of Merchant Vessels.

4. An **Adjuster** is one that adjusts especially an insurance agent who investigates personal or property damage and makes estimates for effecting settlements.

5. A **marine surveyor** is a person who conducts inspections, surveys or examinations of marine vessels to assess, monitor and report on their condition and the products on them, as well as inspects damage caused to both vessels and cargo.

6. A **classification surveyor** inspects ships to make sure that the ship, its components and machinery are built and maintained according to the standards require A classification surveyor inspects ships to make sure that the ship, its components and machinery are built and maintained according to the standards required for their class. d for their class.

7. A **CTO (Combined Transport Operator),** also known as **MTO (Multimodal Transport Operator)** or **ITO (Intermodal Transport Operator)** is a person who transports goods under a single contract, but performs with at least two different means of transport (by rail, sea and road, for example).

8. A **freight forwarder** is a firm specializing in arranging storage and shipping of merchandise on behalf of its shippers. It usually provides a full range of services including: tracking inland transportation, preparation of shipping and export documents, warehousing, booking cargo space, negotiating freight charges, freight consolidation, cargo insurance, and filing of insurance claims.

9. A **ship builider** is a person or company whose job or business is the design and construction of ships.

10. A **Pilot** (도선사) is one who, though not belonging to a ships company, is licensed to conduct a ship into and out of port or through dangerous waters.

Vocabulary Check

✓ Choose the word that best completes each sentence. Change the form of the word if necessary.

1. Smoking cigarettes can __________ bad health.
2. The __________ of two things makes one thing.
3. __________ can mean "very good" or just "very much".
4. If a business __________, it needs more workers.
5. I will stop __________.

Reading Comprehension

✓ Choose the best answer for each question.

1. __________ of the world's trade now moves by sea.

   a. 50%
   b. 80%
   c. 90%
   d. 95%

2. Marine finance and marine insurance are called __________ services.

   a. government
   b. central
   c. support
   d. social

3. Asian ports handle __________ of the world's container shipping.

   a. one fourth
   b. one third
   c. one half
   d. two thirds

4. Companies moved to Asia because of __________ shipping.

   a. cheaper
   b. faster
   c. safer
   d. bigger

5. The biggest shipbuilding company in Korea is __________.

   a. Daewoo
   b. Hyundai
   c. Samsung
   d. Hanjin

6. What factors initiated the modern growth of manufacturing in Asia?

7. What area of maritime economy do you think will grow most in the future?

Did you know?

Maritime environmental professionals work as scientists. They study the earth's oceans in order to understand the impact of human activity upon them. They look for ways to improve the ocean environment through technology. Some work with companies and governments to limit the impact of industrial practices on the world's oceans.

Work Sheet

What are the major facilities for handling containers? What are main transportations for containers?

Unit 10

Cruise Industry

Cruise companies report healthy increases in the number of Asians, including Koreans, getting onboard their ships. They predict the size of the Asian cruise market will expand to 3.7 million by 2017. In this unit, you will learn about the features of cruise ships and the difference between cruise ships and ocean liners.

Oasis of the seas

History of Cruise Ships

Just as "Rome was not built in a day," the cruise ship industry has had a long journey to reach its present state. Then, when did the journey begin, and how has it evolved?

The passenger ship industry **flourished** in the late 1800s and early 1900s, **owing to** the advent of the steam engine and the growing number of American immigrants from Europe. According to Wikipedia, the Peninsular & Oriental Steam Navigation Company based in England introduced passenger cruise services in 1844. The British shipping company White Star Lines, the owner of the Titanic, also began building the first cruise liners in 1849. About that time, many people were crossing the Atlantic by ship, and ships were simply a means of transportation between the North American continent and Europe.

Even before it became well established, the cruise industry went through a terrifying **ordeal** because of World War I, which began in 1914. The cruise industry could not avoid the **calamities** of the war. Normal cruise liners were converted into transports for troops, **refugees**, and war materials, so the cruise industry gradually **faded away** from public view.

After the First World War, the ships that had been **mobilized** for the war were remodeled into cruise liners. As the result of efforts to **bring about** a revival, a new cruise industry in the modern sense was born. While previous cruise ships were only for transportation, they acquired a new image of a hotel on the ocean. On this new type of ship, people could enjoy their voyages in stylish decorated cabins.

■ Vocabulary
- flourish
- owe to
- ordeal
- calamity
- refugee
- faded away
- mobilize
- bring about

However, because of the outbreak of the World War II, the cruise industry **deteriorated** again. Then, in 1958, the first transatlantic jetliner business **dealt** them **another blow**. As a result, most small and medium sized cruise companies closed down. Facing an end to their business, the cruise industry discovered a new opportunity in the Caribbean Sea. Business revived as they added new shipping routes in the Caribbean Sea.

■ Vocabulary
- deteriorate
- dealt another blow

After many complications, the cruise industry became one of the leading businesses around the world. Various kinds of cruises are attracting a variety of people, from the middle class to the rich. Moreover, since the 2000s, thc cruise industry has changed to offer more active experiences and attractions such as casinos, musicals, and parties. Today, some people predict that the cruise industry has boundless potential and anticipate even greater developments.

Vocabulary Check

✓ Choose the word that best completes each sentence. Change the form of the word if necessary.

1. Sleeping too late on exam day is a c_____.
2. Many _____ came here to escape a war.
3. My new job is _____ a letter from my professor.
4. Preparing for the entrance exams was an _____.
5. Some foods _____ quickly.

Reading Comprehension

✓ Choose the best answer for each question.

1. During World War I, many cruise ships were ____________

a. built.
b. destroyed for the metal.
c. converted for military use.
d. sent to Canada.

2. After World War II, the cruise industry suffered because of ____________ _________

a. the high cost of fuel.
b. the high cost of labor.
c. competition from airlines.
d. competition from Asia.

3. Modern cruise ships increased business by becoming ____________

a. fancier.
b. smaller.
c. cheaper.
d. faster.

4. In the 19th century, the cruise industry grew rapidly because of ________ _________

a. war.
b. immigration.
c. government policy.
d. tourism.

5. Modern cruise ships give an experience that is more ____________

a. active.
b. expensive.
c. safe.
d. friendly.

6. In what country did the modern cruise industry begin?

7. Why did the Caribbean become popular instead of some other region?

Did you know?

Cruise ships have morgues. The average cruise ship passenger is middle-aged, and the longer the cruise, the older the median age of its passengers. Cruises lasting longer than a week generally attract senior citizens, who aren't forced home by employment obligations. Unfortunately, when carrying a payload of thousands of elderly people each week, the inevitable happens.

Growth of Cruise Ships

When people travelled across the oceans on ships, the vessels that carried them were called "ocean liners". They were built with a high **freeboard** and strong **plating** to withstand the rough seas of the open ocean. Since the ships were designed for speed and efficiency, cabins were small, uncomfortable, and located inside the hull.

Cruise ships are designed to take passengers on long, slow trips with a maximum of comfort. The biggest change in design from liners is that passenger cabins have been moved from inside the hull to the **superstructure**. This allows every cabin to have a view, and the majority to have a balcony.

These changes have made modern cruise ships look like floating apartment buildings. Although the height of the ships makes them appear top-heavy, they are still stable because their center of mass is low. The upper parts are made of lightweight materials and have large open spaces, while the lower parts hold the heavy things like engines and fuel tanks. Also, the ships are very wide.

The size of cruise ships has grown **tremendously** in the past four decades. In the 1970s, the average size for ships was eight decks and 500 cabins. Now it is over a dozen decks and 1,500 cabins. No rooms had balconies in the 1970s, but now most have them. Not only are cabins roomier, but they have nicer furnishings, more storage space, and all have Internet and flatscreen TVs.

Dining and recreational facilities have greatly expanded. In the 1970s, there was typically a single dining room with fixed mealtimes, plus a few cafes and bars. Now there will be a 24-hour buffet, several restau-

▪ Vocabulary
- freeboard
- plating
- superstructure
- tremendously

rants, and just as many bars. While onboard recreation was once limited to **shuffleboard** and **cribbage**, now you can expect to find nightclubs, theaters, fitness centers, hobby classes, bowling, tennis, and swimming pools with water slides.

- **Vocabulary**
  - shuffleboard
  - cribbage
  - exotic
  - plenty of
  - breeze

Cruise ships sail to **exotic** destinations all over the world. Most cruise destinations are in the Caribbean or Mediterranean seas. Ships destined for those areas are designed for the tropical weather, with **plenty of** shade and open decks that allow the warm **breezes** to pass through.

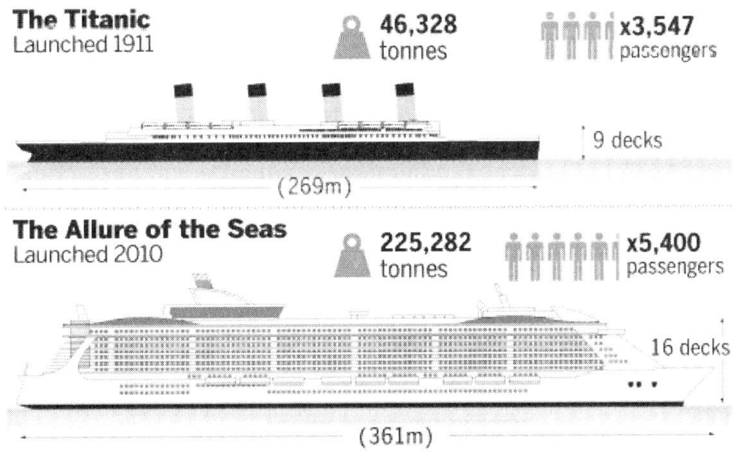

The Royal Caribbean cruise ship Allure of the Seas is available in the Street View of Google Maps.

Vocabulary Check

✓ Choose the word that best completes each sentence. Change the form of the word if necessary

1. __________ is a popular card game.
2. The __________ keeps water from coming onto the ship.
3. __________ things are usually expensive.
4. A gentle __________ is pleasant on a hot day.
5. A __________ is like a building on top of a ship.

Reading Comprehension

✓ Choose the best answer for each question.

1 Ocean liners must be __________ than cruise ships.

a. stronger
b. smaller
c. bigger
d. faster

2. Cruise ships are designed to be as __________ as possible.

a. fast
b. cheap
c. big
d. comfortable

3. Big cruise ships are stable because they are __________.

a. heavy on top
b. light on top
c. long and narrow
d. flat on the bottom

4. In the 1970s, cabins never had __________.

a. closets
b. balconies
c. showers
d. windows

5. Most cruise ships are designed for __________ weather.

a. windy
b. calm
c. tropical
d. sunny

6. Why is an ocean liner not suitable for use as a cruise ship?

7. Why do you think most cruise destinations are in the Caribbean or Mediterranean seas?

Did you know?

The Caribbean is the most popular region for cruises. About half of all cruises are to the Caribbean and nine of the ten most popular cruise ports are there. The second and third most popular regions are Europe and Alaska.

Work Sheet

Busan has a new international cruise terminal built at Busan North Port. What new features does it have? And what is Busan city doing or should do to promote the new terminal?

Unit 11

Maritime Disasters

One of South Korea's deadliest maritime disasters occurred at about 11 miles from Jindo Island on April 16, 2014. Only 172 of the 476 passengers were rescued. Of the 304 confirmed dead or still listed as missing. How could this unbelievable tragedy occur? In this unit, you will learn some natural maritime disasters as well as man-made disasters.

Sewol ferry

Typhoons

What comes to your mind first when you hear such expressions like strong winds, heavy rain, and thunderstorms? Yes, you might answer 'a typhoon' or 'a hurricane' depending on where you live. Typhoon and hurricane are different names for the tropical cyclone. Tropical cyclones are huge **rotating** storms 200 to 2,000 kilometers wide with winds that blow at speeds of more than 100 kilometers per hour. Weather professionals, or **meteorologists,** know them as **tropical** cyclones, but they are called hurricanes in the Caribbean Sea, typhoons in the Pacific Ocean, and cyclones in the Indian Ocean. They occur in both the northern and southern hemispheres. Large ones have destroyed cities and killed hundreds of thousands of people.

Birth of a Giant

We know that tropical cyclones begin over water that is warmer than 27 degrees Celsius, slightly north or south of the earth's equator. Warm, humid air full of water **vapor** moves upward. The earth's rotation causes the growing storm to start to rotate around its center (called the eye). At a certain height, the water vapor condenses, changing to liquid and releasing heat. The heat draws more air and water vapor upward, creating a cycle as air and water vapor rise and liquid water falls. If the cycle speeds up until winds reach 118 kilometers per hour, the storm qualifies as a tropical cyclone.

■ Vocabulary
- rotate
- meteorologist
- tropical
- vapor

Storm surge

Most deaths in tropical cyclones are caused by storm surge. This is a rise in sea level, sometimes seven meters or more, caused by the storm pushing against the ocean's surface. Storm **surge** was to **blame** for the flooding of New Orleans in 2005. The storm surge of Cyclone Nargis in 2008 in Myanmar pushed sea water nearly four meters deep some 40 kilometers in land, resulting in many deaths.

▪ Vocabulary
- surge
- blame

Difficult to predict

The goal is to know when and where the next tropical cyclone will form, but we can't do that yet. The direction and strength of tropical cyclones are also difficult to predict. Three-day forecasts are still off by an average of 280 kilometers. Forecasters do know that storms are of weakened where ocean water is deep and warm, that high waves tend to reduce their force, and that when tropical cyclones move over land, they begin to die.

Modified from Unit 5 Superstorms in *Reading Explorer 2*

Vocabulary Check

✓ Choose the word that best completes each sentence. Change the form of the word if necessary.

1. Water can be a solid, liquid, or __________
2. If you do something wrong, you are __________ for the result.
3. The daily __________ of the earth takes 24 hours.
4. A tsunami causes the sea level to __________.
5. A __________ tries to predict the weather.

Reading Comprehension

✓ Choose the correct answer for each question.

1. Tropical cyclones are called __________ in the Pacific Ocean.

   a. hurricanes
   c. cyclones
   b. typhoons
   d. storms

2. The word "condenses" is closest in meaning to __________.

   a. heat up
   c. start rotating
   b. move higher
   d. become liquid

3. What happens first in the process of storm formation?

   a. Winds reach 118 kilometers per hour.
   b. Warm, humid air moves upward.
   c. Liquid water falls.
   d. Water vapor condenses.

4. Which of the following is closest in meaning to "the direction and strength of tropical storms are difficult to predict, even with computer assistance"?

   a. Despite using computers, it is difficult to know where tropical cyclones will strike next.
   b. Without computers, predicting tropical cyclones is impossible.
   c. Computer assistance removes the difficulty of predicting tropical cyclones
   d. Using computers to predict tropical storms is difficult.

5. In a typhoon, most deaths are caused by __________.

a. wind | c. lighting
b. high sea level | d. traffic accidents

6. What are the different names for Typhoon? And where are they used?

7. What should the government do to prepare for Typhoon?

Did you know?

Weather forecasting as we know it became possible with the invention of the telegraph in 1837. That allowed news of approaching storms to be communicated faster than the weather itself could arrive.

Taean Oil Spill

Residents of Taean, South Chungcheong Province, Korea, are still experiencing financial **setbacks** from the nation's largest-ever oil spill, which hit its shores in December 2007.

An 11,800-ton **barge** owned by Samsung Heavy Industries collided with the Hong Kong-registered 146,000-ton tanker Hebei Spirit in waters off Taean. About 10,850 tons of **crude oil** was spilled into the waters of the Taean National Maritime Park. The oil blackened more than 200 kilometers of beaches and destroyed some 1,000 farms cultivating oysters, **abalone**, seaweed, and fish.

Health is also becoming a critical issue. Oh Bum-jin of the University of Ulsan College of Medicine warned that the case could turn into a chemical disaster since residents and volunteers were exposed to **toxic** substances. "Pregnant women, children and others at the site were exposed to **carcinogens** such as benzene, which could cause **chromosomal** damage," he said. He and other experts warn that the toxicity of the chemicals could cause greater damage in the future. The International Oil Pollution Compensation Fund has decided to pay 322 billion won in compensation but residents claim damage exceeds 1 trillion won. Furthermore, the application for compensation is quite complicated for ordinary citizens, and local news papers reported that a mere 20 percent have applied.

Hundreds of thousands of volunteers have visited Taean, to clean up the nation's worst oil spill. A record number of 1.2 million citizens volunteered to help give life back to the sea.

Thanks to volunteers' support, Taean is recovering at a

■ Vocabulary
- setback
- barge
- crude oil
- abalone
- toxic
- carcinogen
- chromosomal

faster pace than any other oil spill. Seagulls, clams, and other sea creatures are returning to the once-dead sea.

However, even after a year of **toil** and struggle by volunteers and residents, Taean is still **ailing**. The nation has become rather **callous** about the tragedy. There is still oil under the sand on the sea shore and it is affecting the ecosystem, with little being done about it since the volunteers stopped coming.

■ Vocabulary
- toil
- ail
- callous

http://www.koreatimes.co.kr/www/news/nation/2008/12/117_35647.html

Vocabulary Check

✓ Choose the word that best completes each sentence. Change the form of the word if necessary.

1. __________ are chemicals that cause cancer.
2. __________ comes out of the ground.
3. A ship will be damaged if it __________ with something.
4. A __________ is a large boat with a flat bottom.
5. We don't care about something if we are __________.

Reading Comprehension

✓ Choose the correct answer for each question.

1. The main setbacks for people in Taean are __________.

   a. medical
   b. economic
   c. political
   d. social

2. A tanker ship hit a __________.

   a. rock
   b. reef
   c. sand bar
   d. boat

3. __________ in the water has become a health issue.

   a. Sulfur
   b. Carcinogens
   c. Ships
   d. Marine life

4. __________ of the people have applied for compensation money.

   a. All
   b. About 20%
   c. About half
   d. About 80%

5. Most of the people cleaning Taean were __________.

   a. volunteers
   b. from the army
   c. from the government
   d. from the oil company

6. What caused Taean oil spill?

7. If you live in that area, should you be still concerned about health effect?

Did you know?

In general, lighter refined petroleum products such as diesel and gasoline are more likely to mix in the water column and are more toxic to marine life, but tend to evaporate relatively quickly and do not persist long in the environment. Heavier crude or fuel oil, while of less immediate toxicity, can remain on the water surface or stranded on the shoreline for much longer.

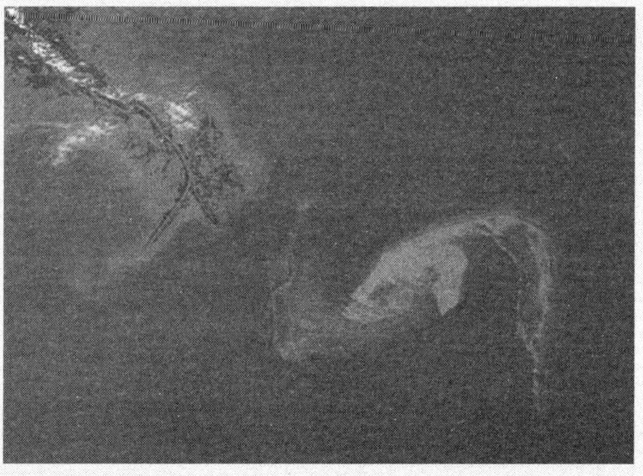

Work Sheet

We see so many maritime disasters throughout the maritime history. What kinds of maritime disasters can you prepare for or can't prepare for?

Unit 12

Maritime Literature

The sea has been more than just a scenic backdrop in Classic Literature. It has played the part of a character since the time of the Odyssey, and the waves are part of what our myths and legends are made of." — American Sea Writing: A Literary Anthology

Moby Dick

ch 42 The Chart

Had you followed Captain Ahab down into his cabin after the **squall** that took place on the night succeeding that wild **ratification** of his purpose with his crew, you would have seen him go to a locker in the **transom**, and bringing out a large wrinkled roll of yellowish sea charts, spread them before him on his screwed-down table. Then seating himself before it, you would have seen him intently study the various lines and shadings which there met his eye; and with slow but steady pencil trace additional courses over spaces that before were blank. At intervals, he would refer to piles of old **log-books** beside him, wherein were set down the seasons and places in which, on various former voyages of various ships, Sperm Whales had been captured or seen. While thus employed, the heavy **pewter** lamp **suspended** in chains over his head, continually rocked with the motion of the ship, and for ever threw shifting **gleams** and shadows of lines upon his wrinkled brow, till it almost seemed that while he himself was marking out lines and courses on the wrinkled charts, some invisible pencil was also tracing lines and courses upon the deeply marked chart of his forehead.

But it was not this night in particular that, in the **solitude** of his cabin, Ahab thus pondered over his charts. Almost every night they were brought out; almost every night some pencil marks were **effaced,** and others were

▪ Vocabulary
- squall
- ratification
- transom
- log–book
- pewter
- suspend
- gleam
- solitude
- efface

substituted. For with the charts of all four oceans before him, Ahab was threading a **maze** of currents and **eddies**, with a view to the more certain accomplishment of that **monomaniac** thought of his soul.

Now, to any one not fully acquainted with the ways of the **leviathans**, it might seem an absurdly hopeless task thus to seek out one solitary creature in the **unhooped** oceans of this planet. But not so did it seem to Ahab, who knew the sets of all tides and currents; and thereby calculating the driftings of the Sperm Whale's food; and, also, calling to mind the regular, **ascertained** seasons for hunting him in particular latitudes could arrive at reasonable **surmises**, almost approaching to certainties, concerning the timeliest day to be upon this or that ground in search of his prey.

■ **Vocabulary**
- substitute
- maze
- eddies
- monomaniac
- leviathans
- unhooped
- ascertain
- surmise

Vocabulary Check

✓ Choose the word that best completes each sentence. Change the form of the word if necessary.

1. An elephant is one of the __________ on land.
2. A __________ is similar to a diary.
3. Some people live alone because they like __________.
4. It rains a lot during a __________.
5. An eraser will __________ pencil writing from paper.

Reading Comprehension

✓ Choose the best answer for each question.

1 Captain Ahab kept his chart in a __________.

a. desk
b. book
c. locker
d. shelf

2. Captain Ahab marked the chart with a __________.

a. pen
b. pencil
c. knife
d. brush

3. The lamp in the cabin was on the __________.

a. ceiling
b. table
c. floor
d. door

4. Captain Ahab worked on his chart __________.

a. twice a day
b. once a day
c. almost every day
d. almost every night

5. Captain Ahab planned to find the whale by following the __________.

a. whale's food
b. whale's family
c. ocean currents
d. trade routes

6. Where did Captain Ahab get the information?

7. What other types of marine life would this strategy be useful for hunting?

Did you know

Blue whales are the largest animals that have ever lived. Although some dinosaurs were about the same length, living in the water allowed blue whales to become as much as three times as heavy.

Kon-Tiki

For a long time we saw no sign of a squid, either on board or in the sea. But then one morning we found a single smaller young squid on the top of the roof of palm leaves. This puzzled us very much. It could not have climbed up there, as the only ink marks were **smeared** in a ring round it in the middle of the roof. Nor had it been dropped by a sea bird, for it was completely **intact** with no **beak** marks. We came to the conclusion that it had been **flung up** on to the roof by a wave which had come on board, but none of those on night watch could remember any such wave that night. As the nights passed, we regularly found more young squids on board, the smallest of them the size of one's middle finger.

One sunny morning we all saw a **glittering shoal** of something which shot up out of the water and flew through the air like large raindrops, while the sea boiled with pursuing dolphins. At first we took it for a shoal of flying fish, for we had already had three different kinds of these on board. But, when they came near and some of them sailed over the raft at a height of four or five feet, one ran straight into Bengt's chest and fell slap on the deck. It was a small squid. Our astonishment was great. When we put it into a sailcloth bucket it kept on taking off and shooting up to the surface, but it did not develop speed enough in the small bucket to get more than half out of the water.

It is a known fact that the squid ordinarily swims on

■ **Vocabulary**

- smear
- intact
- beak
- fling (flung) up
- glitter
- shoal

the principle of the rocket-propelled airplane. It pumps sea water with great force through a closed tube alongside its body and can thus shoot backward in **jerks** at a high speed. With all its **tentacles** hanging behind it in a cluster over its head it becomes **streamlined** like a fish. It has on its sides two round, fleshy folds of skin which are ordinarily used for steering and quiet swimming in the water. But our experience showed that defenseless young squids, which are a favorite food of many large fish, can escape their pursuers by taking to the air in the same way as flying fish. They pump sea water through themselves till they get up a terrific speed, and then they steer up at an angle from the surface by unfolding the pieces of skin like wings. Like the flying fish, they make a glider flight over the waves for as far as their speed can carry them. After that, when we had begun to pay attention, we often saw them sailing along for fifty to sixty yards, singly and in two's and three's.

■ **Vocabulary**
- jerk
- tentacle
- streamline

Vocabulary Check

✓ Choose the word that best completes each sentence. Change the form of the word if necessary.

1. If ink is wet, you can easily __________ it.
2. A ship is __________ so it can move through water easily.
3. The mouth of a bird is called a __________.
4. Diamonds __________ in the light.
5. Something is __________ if it is not broken into pieces.

Reading Comprehension

✓ Choose the best answer for each question.

1. They first found a squid on the __________.

   a. deck
   b. rudder
   c. ropes
   d. roof

2. They thought that a __________ put it there.

   a. bird
   b. octopus
   c. wave
   d. wind

3. All of the squid on the raft were __________.

   a. small
   b. fast
   c. ugly
   d. damaged

4. Squid move by __________.

   a. pushing with their wings
   b. pushing with their tentacles
   c. shooting water
   d. twisting their bodies

5. Squid fly in the air to __________.

   a. find a mate
   b. breathe
   c. travel faster
   d. escape

6. What was the initial conclusion about how the small squids got onboard?

7. Why can the squid fly but not the octopus or jellyfish?

Did you know?

Balsa trees grow extremely fast, so their wood is very light and soft. It is less dense than cork. It is popular for making surfboards and model airplanes.

Work Sheet

There is a large body of literature that revolves around the sea, ocean, or other marine life. Moby Dick and Kon-Tiki you read above are just two of them. Do you know any other sea related-writing, either fiction or non-fiction? Write about it.

Questions & Answers

1a: Origins of the Oceans 136
1b: The Five Oceans 137
2a: Marine Habitats 138
2b: Marine versus Land Mammals 139
3a: Great Explorers 140
3b: Pirates 141
4a: Talking about Ships 143
4b: Nautical Charts 144
5a: History of Ports 145
5b: Port Authorities 146
6a: Law of the Sea 148
6b: Captain Goes down with the Ship 149
7a: Battle of Myeongnyang 150
7b: Coast Guard 151
8a: Aquaculture 152
8b: Food Chain at Sea 154
9a: Container Ships 155
9b: Shipping and the Economy 156
10a: History of Cruise Ships 157
10b: Growth of Cruise Ships 158
11a: Typhoons 159
11b: Taean Oil Spill 161
12a: Moby Dick 162
12b: Kon-Tiki 163

❖ 1a: Origins of the Oceans

Vocabulary Check

1. The center of something may be called the __________. (nucleus)
2. __________ is also called rust. (iron oxide)
3. We breathe the __________. (atmosphere)
4. Something is __________ if it is not all the same. (heterogeneous)
5. The __________ is made of water. (hydrosphere)

Reading Comprehension

1. The Earth was formed in __________. [b]

   a. the explosion of a star
   b. a dust cloud
   c. the collision of asteroids
   d. a gravity well

2. The breakdown of radioactive elements released __________. [a]

   a. energy
   b. tension
   c. gravity
   d. volcanoes

3. __________ sank and became the nucleus. [c]

   a. rocks
   b. light elements
   c. dense elements
   d. water

4. The Earth's surface was cooled by __________. [a]

   a. radiating heat
   b. water vapor
   c. liquid water
   d. volcanic activity

5. __________ became land masses. [c]

a. dry areas
b. large areas
c. areas with lighter crust
d. areas with hills

❖ 1b: The Five Oceans

Vocabulary Check

1. __________ water contains salt. (saline)
2. A liquid will __________ when it becomes cold enough. (solidify)
3. Metal is obtained from processing __________. (ore)
4. A group of islands is an __________. (archipelago)
5. You must be more careful in __________ areas. (hazardous)

Reading Comprehension

1. The oceanic crust is made of __________. [c]

a. hot lava
b. hot water
c. volcanic rock
d. sediment

2. The average depth of the oceans is __________. [b]

a. one kilometer
b. four kilometers
c. five kilometers
d. ten kilometers

3. The Indian ocean is next to __________. [d]

a. East Asia
b. South America & Antarctica
c. South America & Africa
d. Australia & Africa

4. The ocean around Antarctica is the __________. [d]

a. Pacific Ocean
c. Indian Ocean
b. Atlantic Ocean
d. Southern Ocean

5. Studying __________ can help to find petroleum. [a]

a. plate borders
c. ocean currents
b. national borders
d. volcanic currents

❖ 2a: Marine Habitats

Vocabulary Check

1. We get __________ from food. (nutrients)
2. __________ areas are covered by water only part-time. (intertidal)
3. Rain water goes into the ground or into rivers as __________. (runoff)
4. __________ are small fish. (sardines)
5. __________ is a large type of seaweed. (kelp)

Reading Comprehension

1. All marine life needs __________. [d]

a. sunlight
c. plankton
b. warm water
d. nutrients

2. Coral grows only in water that is warm, clear, and __________. [b]

a. deep
c. nutritious
b. shallow
d. calm

3. Most marine life is in __________. [c]

   a. estuaries
   b. deep sea
   c. coastal shelves
   d. intertidal zones

4. The largest marine animals live in the __________. [d]

   a. Pacific Ocean
   b. Indian Ocean
   c. coastal zone
   d. open ocean

5. In the open ocean, the most plentiful life is __________. [a]

   a. plankton
   b. seaweed
   c. fish
   d. whales

❖ 2b: Marine versus Land Mammals

Vocabulary Check

1. Fat from marine mammals is called __________. (blubber)
2. An __________ helps to keep you cool or warm. (insulator)
3. Land mammals use fat just for energy __________. (storage)
4. Deeper under water, you feel more __________. (pressure)
5. Something with less __________ than water will float. (density)

Reading Comprehension

1. Marin mammals get fresh water from __________. [c]

   a. rain
   b. runoff
   c. fish
   d. seaweed

2. Compared to on land, temperature in the ocean __________. [d]

a. is warmer
c. changes more
b. is colder
d. changes less

3. Marine mammals have __________ fat than land mammals. [a]

a. more
c. lighter
b. less
d. denser

4. Land mammals need stronger __________ than marine mammals. [b]

a. fat
c. hair
b. skeletons
d. muscles

5. Ocean water is __________ than the air. [a]

a. denser
c. deeper
b. colder
d. cleaner

❖ 3a: Great Explorers

Vocabulary Check

1. The floor of the ocean is the __________. (sea bed)
2. East-West position is __________. (longitude)
3. __________ is the making of maps. (cartography)
4. A __________ city is next to the sea. (coastal)
5. A __________ is a precise clock. (chronometer)

Reading Comprehension

1. Six thousand years ago, Egyptians sailed in the ________. [d]

   a. North Sea
   b. Indian Ocean
   c. Atlantic Ocean
   d. Mediterranean

2. Captain Cook was looking for ________. [c]

   a. Asia
   b. South America
   c. a southern continent
   d. a route to India

3. Hyecho was a ________. [c]

   a. Chinese travelling to India
   b. Chinese writing in Korean
   c. Korean writing in Chinese
   d. Korean writing about China

4. The first oceanographic research ship was built ________. [b]

   a. of wood
   b. of metal
   c. in England
   d. in France

5. ________ exploration is the study of the ocean floor. [d]

   a. Maritime
   b. Oceanographic
   c. Scientific
   d. Deep sea

❖ 3b: Pirates

Vocabulary Check

1. To __________ someone is to chose a leader. (elect)
2. You must be __________ when driving a car. (sober)
3. Things you got by stealing is __________. (plunder)
4. A __________ is used to store and carry things. (chest)
5. Even sailor can become __________ in rough weather. (seasick)

Reading Comprehension

1. What is the main idea of this reading? [b]
   a. A pirate's life was dangerous but exciting.
   b. Some things we hear about pirates are true.
   c. Modern pirates are similar to 18th-century pirates.
   d. Modern stories about pirates are entirely wrong.

2. On many pirate ships, __________. [d]
   a. men were like slaves
   b. there were several captains
   c. only ex-sailors were allowed
   d. the men shared the money they got

3. "They blew it" means "They __________ the money." [b]
   a. hid
   c. made
   b. spent
   d. saved

4. Which statement would the author probably agree with? [a]

a. Many pirates had a hard life and died young.

b. The appearance of movie pirates is different from reality.

c. A pirate's life wasn't as dangerous as we see in the movies.

d. Many pirates were friendlier than we see in the movies.

5. Pirates believed wearing earrings __________. [b]

a. was fashionable

b. stopped illness

c. brought good luck

d. was only for women

❖ 4a: Talking about Ships

Vocabulary Check

1. The __________ is in the back of a ship. (aft)
2. A boat is moved by motor, sail, or __________. (oar)
3. The lower __________ of a ship are inside. (deck)
4. Water is __________ for life. (crucial)
5. I __________ my captain as "Sir". (refer to)

Reading Comprehension

1. Which of the following is true? [c]

a. Starboard refers to the left side when facing forward.

b. The stern is the front end of the ship.

c. Floors on vessels are called decks.

d. Steps on vessels are called stairs.

2. Submarines are called boats mainly because they __________. [b]

a. are not oceangoing vessels
c. are built for deep water use
b. are small
d. do not use sail for power

3. A boat cannot __________. [a]

a. carry a ship
c. have a sail
b. go in deep water
d. sink

4. Ships show a green light on starboard __________. [d]

a. in a harbor
c. when turning
b. at sea
d. at night

5. Inside a ship, look up to see the __________. [b]

a. deck
c. bulkhead
b. overhead
d. stern

❖ 4b: Nautical Charts

Vocabulary Check

1. It is important that navigation is __________. (accurate)
2. Ships may__________ are created by volcanoes. (seamount)
3. __________ with something in shallow water. (collide)
4. Go north or south to change your __________. (latitude)
5. Unless it is a submarine, a ship on the sea floor is a __________. (shipwreck)

Reading Comprehension

1. A nautical chart needs to show underwater __________. [d]

   a. submarines　　c. fish

   b. pollution　　d. hazards

2. The San Francisco's navigators were not __________ enough. [b]

   a. intelligent　　c. experienced

   b. careful　　d. educated

3. Charts of the Pacific Ocean may be up to __________ years old. [c]

   a. 100　　c. 300

   b. 200　　d. 400

4. Modern hydrographic surveying is more __________. [a]

   a. precise　　c. complete

   b. expensive　　d. difficult

5. It is dangerous to expect that GPS navigation is more __________. [c]

   a. expensive　　c. accurate

   b. affordable　　d. popular

❖ 5a: History of Ports

Vocabulary Check

1. Something __________ is not separate. (integral)
2. A __________ job does not have a regular schedule. (casual)
3. People usually do not return to something that they __________. (abandon)
4. A __________ is where paths of travel meet. (node)
5. People enter a __________ for protection. (fortification)

Reading Comprehension

1. In history, ports were mainly __________. [a]

   a. international markets
   b. fish markets
   c. travel centers
   d. construction centers

2. In modern times, ports became mainly __________. [b]

   a. construction centers
   b. transport centers
   c. more efficient
   d. more crowded

3. Growing ports also caused workers' __________ to grow. [d]

   a. incomes
   b. happiness
   c. health
   d. neighborhoods

4. Larger ships required ports with __________. [c]

   a. more workers
   b. lower taxes
   c. deeper water
   d. newer equipment

5. Technological changes have __________ ports. [a]

a. altered
c. isolated
b. preserved
d. reduced

❖ 5b: Port Authorities

Vocabulary Check

1. Container ships carry __________. (freight)
2. Beauty is a result of __________ qualities. (aesthetic)
3. Things are kept in __________. (warehouses)
4. Boats are usually kept at the __________. (waterfront)
5. A __________ makes and enforces rules. (commission)

Reading Comprehension

1. Port authorities are created by __________. [d]

a. businesses
c. citizen groups
b. ship companies
d. governments

2. "Self-supporting" means that they don't get money from the __________. [c]

a. businesses
c. government
b. ships
d. customers

3. Ports must grow because __________ keep growing. [a]

a. ships
c. people
b. cities
d. oceans

4. A port authority will use another company to provide __________. [b]

   a. security
   b. banking
   c. licensing
   d. ship inspection

5. Port authorities help the economy by __________ new companies. [a]

   a. attracting
   b. starting
   c. promoting
   d. financing

❖ 6a: Law of the Sea

Vocabulary Check

1. __________ rights are not shared. (exclusive)
2. A visa gives you __________ to enter a country. (permission)
3. Minerals and oil come from __________ the ocean floor. (mining)
4. __________ in the ocean kills much marine life. (pollution)
5. The land and water claimed by a country is its __________. (territory)

Reading Comprehension

1. Historically, the oceans were ruled by __________. [c]

   a. kings
   b. tradition
   c. force
   d. accident

2. Countries claimed territorial waters to protect their __________. [b]

   a. trade
   b. fishing
   c. water
   d. navy

3. We now search the ocean for more __________. [d]

a. pollution
b. coal
c. diamonds
d. oil

4. A country's EEZ gives it __________ economic rights. [c]

a. primary
b. simple
c. sole
d. traditional

5. Foreign ships can freely __________ in an EEZ. [a]

a. travel
b. fish
c. trade
d. mine

❖ 6b: Captain Goes down with the Ship

Vocabulary Check

1. To kill someone by carelessness is __________. (manslaughter)
2. People prefer to __________ danger. (flee from)
3. People will usually __________ a bad person. (revile)
4. __________ is not doing what you should do. (negligence)
5. __________ ideas are not modern. (archaic)

Reading Comprehension

1. The Costa Concordia sank __________ the Sewol. [a]

a. two years before
b. one year before
c. two months before
d. two months after

2. Passenger ships are required to practice the __________ plan. [d]

   a. turning
   b. loading
   c. travel
   d. evacuation

3. In the 1800s, captains were __________ for staying on sinking ships. [c]

   a. stupid
   b. famous
   c. praised
   d. criticized

4. In America, a ship captain must leave the ship __________. [b]

   a. when it sinks
   b. after all passengers
   c. to help passengers
   d. in a lifeboat

5. Captain Schettino was charged with __________. [b]

   a. cowardice
   b. manslaughter
   c. murder
   d. theft

❖ 7a: Battle of Myeongnyang

Vocabulary Check

1. A ship will just __________ without power. (drift)
2. A __________ is a narrow area of sea between two land areas. (strait)
3. An __________ story is not short or simple. (epic)
4. Something __________ is not imported. (home-grown)
5. Your __________ salary is before taxes and expenses. (gross)

Reading Comprehension

1. Yi Sun-sin chose Myeongnyang for the battle because __________. [b]

   a. it was close to his port
   b. it had currents that changed direction
   c. it had a lot of room for moving
   d. it had shallow water

2. At Myeongnyang, most Japanese died from __________. [d]

   a. arrows
   b. cannon
   c. fire
   d. drowning

3. Yi Sun-sin's final battle was at __________. [d]

   a. Busan
   b. Ulsan
   c. Myeongnyang
   d. Noryang

4. Yi Sun-sin was killed by a __________. [c]

   a. spear
   b. fire
   c. bullet
   d. arrow

5. The Japanese defeated the Russians at __________. [a]

   a. Tsushima
   b. Tokushima
   c. Namhae
   d. Vladivostok

❖ 7b: Coast Guard

Vocabulary Check

1. A tsunami is one of the biggest maritime __________. (disasters)
2. The main __________ of the Coast Guard is to protect. (purpose)
3. People try to __________ illegal things into a country. (smuggle)
4. A criminal will be __________ a crime. (charged with)
5. A navigation light can be on land or __________. (offshore)

Reading Comprehension

1. A coast guard patrols a country's __________. [c]

   a. rivers　　c. EEZ
   b. lakes　　d. ports

2. A coast guard does not help __________. [c]

   a. sinking ferries　　c. travel agents
   b. lost fishermen　　d. drowning swimmers

3. The US Coast Guard was created to regulate __________. [b]

   a. fishing　　c. pirates
   b. imports　　d. travel

4. A coast guard does not help prevent __________. [c]

   a. smuggling　　c. tourism
   b. oil spills　　d. accidents

5. A coast guard does not help look for lost __________. [d]

a. ships
b. swimmers
c. airplanes
d. trains

❖ 8a: Aquaculture

Vocabulary Check

1. Water on the __________ is not very deep. (coastal shelf)
2. Growing land plants and animals is not part of __________. (aquaculture)
3. To __________ is to go under the water. (submerge)
4. __________ water comes from below. (upwelling)
5. I graduated and __________ got a job. (subsequently)

Reading Comprehension

1. Wild fisheries are not found in __________. [c]

a. oceans
b. lakes
c. clouds
d. rivers

2. Most capture fisheries are located in __________. [a]

a. costal shelves
b. warm water
c. deep water
d. harbors

3. Aquaculture is the __________ of fish. [d]

a. capturing
b. releasing
c. eating
d. growing

4. __________ seaweed in North Korea comes from farms. [d]

a. No
b. Some
c. Most
d. All

5. The healthy oils in fish meat comes from __________. [b]

a. plankton
b. plants
c. exercise
d. salt water

❖ 8b: Food Chain at Sea

Vocabulary Check

1. Traditional gardens may have __________ in the water. (carp)
2. An __________ will begin something. (instigator)
3. Something __________ is easy to break. (fragile)
4. A __________ eats other animals. (predator)
5. Pollution can __________ marine life. (endanger)

Reading Comprehension

1. Species of fish survive if they are the __________. [c]

a. largest
b. fastest
c. fittest
d. smartest

2. Overfishing can cause __________. [b]

a. pollution
b. species imbalance
c. high prices
d. trade imbalance

3. If too many fish are caught, they are unable to __________. [a]

a. compete
b. migrate
c. reproduce
d. swim

4. After El Nino, Peru's __________ population was reduced. [c]

a. squid
b. tuna
c. anchovy
d. shark

5. Protesters want to protect __________ species of fish. [c]

a. popular
b. delicious
c. endangered
d. fittest

❖ 9a: Container Ships

Vocabulary Check

1. Voting is the __________ of democratic government. (backbone)
2. Ships usually carry people or __________. (freight)
3. Trains are loaded at a __________. (railyard)
4. A __________ container saves money. (reusable)
5. An envelope is __________ to protect the contents. (sealed)

Reading Comprehension

1. Shipping containers were first designed for __________ use. [c]

a. storage
b. railroad
c. truck
d. maritime

2. Shipping containers are made mostly of __________. [b]

a. aluminum
c. iron
b. steel
d. wood

3. After it is sealed, a container is opened only by the __________. [a]

a. customer
c. transporter
b. customs agent
d. dock workers

4. Large container ships make transport __________. [c]

a. faster
c. cheaper
b. cleaner
d. harder

5. Container ships may become too __________ to be used everywhere. [d]

a. many
c. old
b. expensive
d. big

❖ 9b: Shipping and the Economy

Vocabulary Check

1. Smoking cigarettes can __________ bad health. (contribute to)
2. The __________ of two things makes one thing. (fusion)
3. __________ can mean "very good" or just "very much". (terrific)
4. If a business __________, it needs more workers. (expands)
5. I will stop __________. (at one point or another)

Reading Comprehension

1. __________ of the world's trade now moves by sea. [c]

a. 50%
b. 80%
c. 90%
d. 95%

2. Marine finance and marine insurance are called __________ services. [c]

a. government
b. central
c. support
d. social

3. Asian ports handle __________ of the world's container shipping. [b]

a. one fourth
b. one third
c. one half
d. two thirds

4. Companies moved to Asia because of __________ shipping. [a]

a. cheaper
b. faster
c. safer
d. bigger

5. The biggest shipbuilding company in Korea is __________. [b]

a. Daewoo
b. Hyundai
c. Samsung
d. Hanjin

❖ 10a: History of Cruise Ships

Vocabulary Check

1. Sleeping too late on exam day is a _____. (calamity)
2. Many _____ came here to escape a war. (refugees)
3. My new job is _____ a letter from my professor. (owed to)
4. Preparing for the entrance exams was an _____. (ordeal)
5. Some foods _____ quickly. (deteriorate)

Reading Comprehension

1. During World War I, many cruise ships were _____ [c]

   a. built.
   b. destroyed for the metal.
   c. converted for military use.
   d. sent to Canada.

2. After World War II, the cruise industry suffered because of _____ [b]

   a. the high cost of fuel.
   b. the high cost of labor
   c. competition from airlines.
   d. competition from Asia.

3. Modern cruise ships increased business by becoming _____ [a]

   a. fancier.
   b. smaller.
   c. cheaper.
   d. faster.

4. In the 19th century, the cruise industry grew rapidly because of _____ [b]

   a. war.
   b. immigration.
   c. government policy.
   d. tourism.

5. Modern cruise ships give an experience that is more _____ [a]

a. active.
b. expensive.
c. safe.
d. friendly.

❖ 10b: Growth of Cruise Ships

Vocabulary Check

1. __________ is a popular card game. (cribbage)
2. The __________ keeps water from coming onto the ship. (freeboard)
3. __________ things are usually expensive. (exotic)
4. A gentle __________ is pleasant on a hot day. (breeze)
5. A __________ is like a building on top of a ship. (superstructure)

Reading Comprehension

1. Ocean liners must be __________ than cruise ships. [a]

a. stronger
b. smaller
c. bigger
d. faster

2. Cruise ships are designed to be as __________ as possible. [d]

a. fast
b. cheap
c. big
d. comfortable

3. Big cruise ships are stable because they are __________. [b]

a. heavy on top
b. light on top
c. long and narrow
d. flat on the bottom

4. In the 1970s, cabins never had __________. [b]

a. closets
c. showers
b. balconies
d. windows

5. Most cruise ships are designed for __________ weather. [c]

a. windy
c. tropical
b. calm
d. sunny

❖ 11a: Typhoons

Vocabulary Check

1. Water can be a solid, liquid, or __________. (vapor)
2. If you do something wrong, you are __________ for the result. (blamed)
3. The daily __________ of the earth takes 24 hours. (rotation)
4. A tsunami causes the sea level to __________. (surge)
5. A __________ tries to predict the weather. (meteorologist)

Reading Comprehension

1. Tropical cyclones are called __________ in the Pacific Ocean. [b]

a. hurricanes
c. cyclones
b. typhoons
d. storms

2. "Condenses" in this reading means to __________. [d]

a. heat up
c. start rotating
b. move higher
d. become liquid

3. What happens first in the process of storm formation? [b]

   a. Winds reach 118 km per hour.

   b. Warm, humid air moves upward.

   c. Liquid water falls.

   d. Water vapor condenses.

4. Which of the following is closest in meaning to "the direction and strength of tropical storms are difficult to predict, even with computer assistance"? [a]

   a. Despite using computers, it is difficult to know where tropical cyclones will strike next.

   b. Without computers, predicting tropical cyclones is impossible.

   c. Computer assistance removes the difficulty of predicting tropical cyclones

   d. Using computers to predict tropical storms is difficult.

5. In a typhoon, most deaths are caused by __________. [b]

   a. wind

   b. high sea level

   c. lighting

   d. traffic accidents

❖ 11b: Taean Oil Spill

Vocabulary Check

1. __________ are chemicals that cause cancer. (carcinogens)
2. __________ comes out of the ground. (crude oil)
3. A ship will be damaged if it __________ with something. (collides)
4. A __________ is a large boat with a flat bottom. (barge)
5. We don't care about something if we are __________. (callous)

Reading Comprehension

1. The main setbacks for people in Taean are __________. [b]

a. medical
b. economic
c. political
d. social

2. A tanker ship hit a __________. [d]

a. rock
b. reef
c. sand bar
d. boat

3. __________ in the water has become a health issue. [b]

a. Sulfur
b. Carcinogens
c. Ships
d. Marine life

4. __________ of the people have applied for compensation money. [b]

a. All
b. About 20%
c. About half
d. About 80%

5. Most of the people cleaning Taean were __________. [a]

a. volunteers
b. from the army
c. from the government
d. from the oil company

❖ 12a: Moby Dick

Vocabulary Check

1. An elephant is one of the __________ on land. (leviathans)
2. A __________ is similar to a diary. (log-book)
3. Some people live alone because they like __________. (solitude)
4. It rains a lot during a __________. (squall)
5. An eraser will __________ pencil writing from paper. (efface)

Reading Comprehension

1. Captain Ahab kept his chart in a __________. [c]

   a. desk
   b. book
   c. locker
   d. shelf

2. Captain Ahab marked the chart with a __________. [b]

   a. pen
   b. pencil
   c. knife
   d. brush

3. The lamp in the cabin was on the __________. [a]

   a. ceiling
   b. table
   c. floor
   d. door

4. Captain Ahab worked on his chart __________. [d]

   a. twice a day
   b. once a day
   c. almost every day
   d. almost every night

5. Captain Ahab planned to find the whale by following the __________. [a]

a. whale's food
b. whale's family
c. ocean currents
d. trade routes

❖ 12b: Kon-Tiki

Vocabulary Check

1. If ink is wet, you can easily __________ it. (smear)
2. A ship is __________ so it can move through water easily. (streamlined)
3. The mouth of a bird is called a __________. (beak)
4. Diamonds __________ in the light. (glitter)
5. Something is __________ if it is not broken into pieces. (intact)

Reading Comprehension

1. They first found a squid on the __________. [d]

a. deck
b. rudder
c. ropes
d. roof

2. They thought that a __________ put it there. [c]

a. bird
b. octopus
c. wave
d. wind

3. All of the squid on the raft were __________. [a]

a. small
b. fast
c. ugly
d. damaged

4. Squid move by _________. [c]

   a. pushing with their wings
   b. pushing with their tentacles
   c. shooting water
   d. twisting their bodies

5. Squid fly in the air to _________. [d]

   a. find a mate
   b. breathe
   c. travel faster
   d. escape

Maritime Topics for
English Learners

지은이 류미림
펴낸이 조경희
펴낸곳 경문사
펴낸날 2015년 12월 1일 1판 1쇄
등 록 1979년 11월 9일 제313-1979-23호
주 소 121-818, 서울특별시 마포구 와우산로 174
전 화 (02)332-2004 팩스 (02)336-5193
이메일 kyungmoon@kyungmoon.com

값 12,000원

ISBN 978-89-6105-953-4